# Death and Life in America

Biomedicine and Biblical Healing
Second Edition

*Raymond Downing*

FOREWORD BY
*Farr Curlin*

CASCADE *Books* · Eugene, Oregon

DEATH AND LIFE IN AMERICA
Biomedicine and Biblical Healing. Second edition.

Cascade Books
An Imprint of Wipf and Stock Publishers
199 W. 8th Ave., Suite 3
Eugene, OR 97401

www.wipfandstock.com

PAPERBACK ISBN: 978-1-7252-5968-3
HARDCOVER ISBN: 978-1-7252-5969-0
EBOOK ISBN: 978-1-7252-5970-6

## *Cataloguing-in-Publication data:*

Names: Downing, Raymond, author. | Curlin, Farr, foreword.

Title: Death and life in America : biomedincine and biblical healing. Second
    edition / Raymond Downing ; foreword by Farr Curlin.

Description: Eugene, OR: Cascade Books, 2021. | Includes bibliographical
    references.

Identifiers: ISBN 978-1-7252-5969-0 (paperback). | ISBN 978-1-7252-5969-0
    (hardcover). | ISBN 978-1-7252-5970-6 (ebook).

Subjects: Religion and Medicine—United States. | Pastoral theology. |
    Health—Religious aspects—Christianity.

Classification: LCSH: BT732.5 D69 2021 (print). | BT732.5 (ebook).

To my Mother
and to Emmanuel

# Contents

# Foreword

RAY DOWNING HAD THE gift of prophecy, and like many of the prophets of old, Ray wandered in the "wilderness," practicing medicine in East Africa, outside the centers of power. From that vantage Ray could see what we in the West have not had eyes to see.

I met Ray in 2004, when he introduced himself after I, as a newly minted clinical investigator from the University of Chicago, presented data from a study I had done of Christian clinicians working in underserved communities in the United States. Those clinicians saw themselves as called by God to their work, but many were discouraged and even bewildered. They found themselves wondering whether they should go on in their work. Why would that be?

One might think that these clinicians struggled with the sacrifices they had made—earning less money, enjoying less social prestige, working longer hours, living in less resourced neighborhoods, being associated with "the poor." But as I listened, I heard something else: as these Christians labored to bring the best of today's medicine—what Ray here calls *biomedicine*—to those who lacked access to it, they lived with a gnawing sense that they were not doing their patients much good.

Could it be, I asked the audience, that Christian clinicians should stop taking it for granted that faithful practices of medicine involve delivering evidence-based medicine to those who lack access to it? Must they instead work to discern which practices offered by biomedicine are actually good?—which align with the truth about who God is and what we are as human beings?

Ray, it turns out, had been thinking about this for years, and so began a friendship of letters in which I have been his student. From his vantage as a Western physician practicing medicine in East Africa, Ray observed the cultural power of biomedicine to tell people what is going on, what they need, and how the imperial biomedicine will save them from illness and death. In the contexts in which he worked, he also saw that the emperor's clothes often were threadbare, if not entirely transparent.

Moreover, as a man who spent his life dwelling with God, immersed in the Scriptures, Ray saw that biomedicine was among the *powers and principalities* that the apostle Paul spoke about, powers that govern our world, sharing in God's creative goodness but fallen and corrupted by sin. As a corrupted power, biomedicine claims powers over life and death that it does not have, and it claims authority to govern our lives that we should reject.

When the biblical prophets spoke, sometimes they told the future, but more often they spoke the truth that the people had forgotten. They exposed the pretenses and lies of the powers and principalities of their time, and they called out God's people for their infidelity and idolatry—their patterns of going along with and being corrupted by the practices of those who do not fear or know God. Ray likewise calls Christians today to remember what we have forgotten and to open our eyes to the way we are treating biomedicine and bio-life with a reverence and fear that belongs to God alone.

In his life, death, and resurrection, Jesus unmasked and exposed the powers and principalities for what they are—empty ways of attempting to control our worlds and to avoid suffering and death. In this book Ray takes us back to a number of Jesus' healing encounters to help us see the stark differences between the healing that Christ brings and what biomedicine offers. If you are like me, you may experience scales falling from your eyes as Ray leads you through these stories and points to their cosmic significance.

This book does not simply deconstruct biomedicine, much less demonize it. Rather, it helps us to appreciate and make wise use of the often wondrous resources that biomedicine offers, without foolishly swallowing biomedicine's pretenses to deliver us from illness and death. Ray helps us to discern how to make use of biomedicine's power to manipulate mechanisms without confusing that power with the power to heal. He helps us to discern uses of biomedicine that free us from those that hold us captive.

Jesus told us plainly that if we would live we must die, that those who hold on to their bio-lives and their possessions and their need to be in control will lose not only that which they hold on to but also the life that their souls truly long for. In this book Ray shows us how complicit we have become in the contemporary world's vain pretense of autonomy—of being able to stay in control and live apart from God. We have become complicit not least through our efforts to preserve our bio-life through a biomedicine and bioethics in which God is beside the point. He writes to help us remember that only God can carry our diseases, and only God ultimately heals.

If Ray is right, Christians today will have to practice selective renunciation with respect to biomedicine if we are to free ourselves of its claim to god-like power over our lives. We must renounce biomedicine's authority to tell us how to live. We must renounce what it offers when what it offers does not in fact heal. And we must renounce our idolatry of the bio-life that biomedicine promises to preserve. As Christians detach from simple allegiance to biomedicine, they will need to recover their capacity to suffer, with one another, and to live without being captive to the fear of death.

Throughout his own long illness from prostate cancer, Ray demonstrated that capacity to suffer, and on January 20, 2020, he died in the Lord, just after completing the book you hold in your hands. Two months before he died, I wrote to him:

> Ray, You are finishing well. May our Lord grant you your heart's deepest desires as you live out your last days, and may they be multiplied for the sake of your family and

friends and those who will receive grace through your blessings and prayers and work. I have a hunch [that] your writing will be discovered and appreciated more in the coming decade than it has been so far. And of course all of this is straw, as Aquinas said, compared to the firm reality of Christ that is growing ever firmer in you.

Like all true prophets, Ray Downing prayed and worked to help God's people distinguish the firm reality of God from the empty promises of all that is not God. As Christians wake up to that task in the context of biomedicine, they will find this book an invaluable resource.

Farr Curlin, MD
Josiah Trent Professor of Medical Humanities
Co-Director, Theology, Medicine, and Culture Initiative
Duke University

# Preface

I could not have analyzed medicine without bringing into this analysis my passionate attempt to understand a little bit of the Gospels ...[1]

The condition at the end of time which today takes its form in our thoughts, feelings, and perceptions—can only be grasped by those who unequivocally believe in the reality of the Gospel.[2]

IVAN ILLICH

THIS IS A BOOK about modern biomedical health care, about suffering and healing, death and life. In this study I have chosen to use biblical language for several reasons. First, since suffering and healing are essentially spiritual, spiritual language is appropriate. Second, since modern biomedicine is very powerful, we need language that enables us to think and write about power. Using purely secular or scientific language blunts the whole discourse; using biblical language provides more tools and concepts to enter the spiritual realities of death and life, and to help describe and analyze the power of biomedicine. On one level, then, this study is a dialogue between biblical healing and biomedicine.

But a more immediate reason for using biblical language than even these two is Ivan Illich. One of the twentieth century's most

1. Illich, *Rivers*, 121.
2. Duden, "Ivan Illich," 18.

insightful critics of modern biomedicine, Illich felt that Western medicine could not be understood in any other way. His close associate Barbara Duden, a historian of the body, introduced the role of Illich's faith by commenting on his discussion of "the flesh." She said, "for him the flesh orients one inexorably toward the Incarnation, toward the mystery in the world of his faith, and ultimately toward the Cross."[3] "His faith in the Incarnation . . . was the prime mover in all of Ivan's thinking and doing."[4]

None of this was apparent in his 1976 landmark book *Medical Nemesis: The Expropriation of Health*. Yet for a quarter century after the publication of that book, Illich continued to write and speak about health care, developing more fully the biblical roots of his analysis. It is those roots that I am attempting to explore more fully in this book. Consequently none of what will be found below is intended as a departure from or addition to biblical faith.

I began this study by reading everything I could find by Illich on health care written since *Medical Nemesis*, and then rereading an early book by one of his mentors, Jacques Ellul—*The Presence of the Kingdom*, published first in 1948. Throughout that book, but especially in chapters 1 and 4, Ellul emphasizes the need for thinking Christians (he calls them Christian intellectuals) to think through the implications of the Christian faith for their occupations. Since those doing this kind of reflecting are unlikely to be professionally trained theologians, he calls the result of their thinking "practical theology" rather than "speculative theology."

This theological "layman," he says, "must think out, very clearly, his situation as a Christian at work in the world, . . . he has a very clear function to fulfill, and no one can take his place."[5] This is my rationale for reflecting on biblical texts despite my lack of formal theological training. I have also relied on several works by another disciple of Ellul, William Stringfellow. After finishing my first draft, I found that Ellul, in a brief 1947 article, "Biblical

3. Duden, "Quest," 220.
4. Duden, "Ivan Illich," 17.
5. Ellul, *Presence*, 96–97.

Healing and Biomedicine," had already anticipated several of the themes developed here.[6]

Another incentive to write this book was some correspondence with Fr. Emmanuel Katongole, including this email:

> What we are talking about is not only the Power (with capital P) of Western science to name what is going on, but the Power of Western economics and Western medicine to be the savior . . . I find the ethical debates . . . both superficial and misleading as long as they do not question the very power of Western medicine. Of course questioning this power is a dangerous game . . . Medicine and medical technology is the way through which the West is going to exercise hegemony in the 21st century. Forget about the computer revolution of three decades ago. Asia and India have already overtaken America in this regard. Now it is through its medicines and pharmaceutics that the West (America pre-eminently) hopes to control the souls, minds and bodies of the world![7]

On first reading this may sound like the ravings of a paranoid conspiracy theorist. On further reflection, I think these are simple statements of fact; I hope this book helps to explain why.

Such a bold indictment requires a clarification right at the beginning. I recognize there can be a significant difference between Western medicine and the people who practice it. Some of its practitioners are deeply compassionate people who care about, and help heal, their patients. Others are simply servants of the technology. This book is not primarily about the practitioners of Western medicine; it is rather about Western medicine itself and its effects on society, which of course includes both doctors and patients.

This book is titled *Death and Life in America*; it is a sequel to my first book on biomedicine, *Suffering and Healing in America*. I used the word *America* in the same way William Stringfellow referred to America in *An Ethic for Christians and Other Aliens*

---

6. Ellul, "Biblical Positions."

7. Personal communication with the author, 2005.

*in a Strange Land*—as an example of the biblical Babylon. "Babylon," he wrote, "represents the essential version of the demonic in triumph in a nation. Babylon is thus a parable for Nazi Germany. And Babylon is thus a parable for America."[8] My goal is to follow Stringfellow's use of Babylon, not explore medicine in the Babylon of the ancient Near East.

Finally, the dedication of this book is to my mother. I would like to tell here the story of her dying, for it just cracks open the door to the present discussion and enables us to peek into the strange mixture of human life, technological "healing," and meaning.

Sometime in her eighties, my mother stopped talking. Not all at once, of course; at first she had trouble finding the right words, then trouble finding even the right sounds. She could still hum, though, and for a long time made the same facial expressions I remember from years ago. Her face was still a face I recognized and she could still laugh, but as her mind stopped working, so did her language.

Words were always important to her: she was a teacher. She studied music education at New York University; then, on her own, she set off for a teaching stint in the coal fields of West Virginia. She talked, she sang—and she was strong: pictures of her before she married show a city girl: pretty, pleasant, but not delicate.

She loved to tell stories, stories that could get kind of long . . . but she also listened well to my stories, even when my father thought them a bit odd. We weren't a reading family—the books from my parents' college days collected dust on the shelves—but we were a talking family, all of us. In-laws still find it frustrating to be around my sisters and me when we get talking. But I detected no gender imbalance in who dominated the conversations; as I said, my mother was strong.

Then my mother stopped talking. Not all people who lose their minds stop talking, and I have wondered what stopped her.

When I was in high school, my mother got breast cancer, and I'm not sure I knew the full significance of that diagnosis then. She had had other surgery before, and all I knew was that surgery was

8. Stringfellow, *Ethic*, 33.

a big deal. But my dad knew—knew it could kill her. It was in the summer, my sisters were away at camp, and my mom was already in the hospital.

Dad found me in the family room one day and asked that I pray with him. Now we no longer prayed together at night and I was a bit out of shape, but it seemed pretty important to him. So we prayed: nothing very long or emotional, because that's not the way we did things. But we were on our knees, and when we got up, there just might have been a tear in Dad's eye. And that was all.

Well, not quite all. Mom left the hospital without any cancer, and I was left with the haunting memory of a father who sought me out because he needed to pray with me, and a Father who heard that prayer.

That was a technological healing: My mom had a radical mastectomy, followed by radiotherapy, and forty years later she was still alive. It was also a spiritual healing: My dad and I prayed, and my mom prayed. She wasn't finished with life, she said, and with earning money to put us through college; she had faith that God would heal her. She didn't even seem that frightened to me.

In those days she had a lot on her platter with a full-time job and a full-time family. She didn't seem stressed to us, though—just busy, but never too busy to hear one of our stories or tell one of hers. Even though the stories weren't hilarious, we laughed a lot in our family (besides talking a lot), often at the dinner table—sometimes laughed till it hurt. My dad said laughter aids digestion, he'd learned that in health class in school. When my mom finally retired, my sister concluded that she must have been under some stress while she worked, because she became even more mellow and more laid-back at home.

She, like my dad, remained physically healthy—except for her arthritis. It bent her fingers every which way and must have ached, but she never broadcast the pain. It was the difficulty walking that finally pushed her to seek something more than pain pills. A surgeon discussed with her a knee joint replacement, though he seemed to want to postpone the surgery as long as possible, since the artificial joint itself would eventually wear out. She said she wanted to walk *now*, when she still had everything else working well enough. She got the knee at age sixty-nine—but this time she was afraid, I thought, more afraid than before her breast surgery. It seemed to me less was at stake—"just" a limb versus her life. Was it just that she was older?

The surgery was successful—as was the replacement of the replacement ten years later. She stayed alive and stayed able to walk because of what modern biomedicine offered her. Then her brain wore out.

For a while, she was still my mom—her smile, her expressions—but eventually even those ties with the mother we knew drifted away. My sister said the mom she knew had been gone for a long time; now she was taking care of somebody else. It was a fine nursing home she moved into: nice grounds, pleasant staff, music, pictures, activities—and above all no pretensions of biomedical healing. No, she wasn't with her family, but she didn't know that. When she lay on her bed and looked up, it's as if she was looking, not at the ceiling, but through it. She, and we, waited. . . and finally she died.

⤳

So why did she stop talking? Neurology can help us understand the mechanism of speech and how my mother lost it, but not everyone with dementia loses the ability to talk. My mother did. Why?

All of us connect to the world with our five senses—and the tongue, which tastes, also talks. Talking isn't one of those senses, but it is a way we connect, a way we "taste" the world. We talk, and then watch and listen to see how we were heard; we listen, and then respond with words. My mother talked freely, but not excessively. Her speech was not a way to control but to engage; it was a way for her to touch someone, and be touched in return.

When biomedicine was able to remove her diseased breast, she kept talking; when it repaired her diseased knee, she kept talking. But when biomedicine could not heal her diseased mind, she became mute. It's as if she renounced the means of connecting with the world when she no longer understood that world or had anything to offer it.

I am well aware that the conventional explanation for my mother's mutism is exactly the opposite—that her diseased brain took away what she would have preferred to maintain; that she did not actively renounce talking but passively suffered the theft of her speech by her disease. I am speaking here not of mechanism but of metaphor, of meaning. I am, from within the reductionism of biomedicine, saying that mechanism is *not* all there is. I offer this book as a very small hint, an introduction, to what else there might be.

# Acknowledgments

To THOSE WHO HAVE helped me as I wrote this book, I offer my sincere thanks. When you accepted *Suffering and Healing in America*, Gillian, I realized the need for this sequel. Your email from Kampala, Emmanuel, was invaluable. Conversations with you, Patrick, Farr, and Tony, were all very important as I began writing. The CD dictionary and concordance you sent, Mary Ellen and Nancy, were vital aids as I researched.

Researching recent important but not *very* famous thinkers allowed me contact with those who knew them. Thanks Barbara for the Illich bibliography, and Joyce for the Ellul articles on medicine—and Mary Kay for the translation from French.

I learned long ago that completing the manuscript only means completing the first draft. Your initial comments on it, Emmanuel, Tom, Tom, Michael, and several outside readers from Herald Press were all vital in helping me write subsequent drafts. And you who read the subsequent drafts, Jan, Elizabeth, Timothy, MaryCatherine, and Kristopher, ensured that there would be yet more drafts.

Thank you too, Levi, Herald Press, and Wipf and Stock for believing in this project.

# *Part One*

# Introduction

Death lives with us everyday. Indeed our ways of dying are our ways
of living. Or should I say our ways of living are our ways of dying?

—ZAKES MDA, *WAYS OF DYING*, 1995

## 1

# Two Kingdoms

OVER HALF A CENTURY ago, during World War II, four children in England were sent to stay in a large old house in the country to avoid being in London during the bombings. While playing in the house on a rainy day, they discovered a spare room containing a large wooden wardrobe. One day, trying to avoid the annoying housekeeper, they slipped into the wardrobe—and found themselves in Narnia.

They grew up in Narnia, eventually becoming kings and queens there, and years later they returned to England, emerging from the wardrobe just missing the annoying housekeeper they were trying to avoid.

A year later the same four children were sitting together on a railway platform in England on their way to boarding school when they were somehow all pulled back to Narnia. They stayed there for months, and then returned to the railway platform before their train had arrived.

After the war was over, the two younger children returned with their cousin to Narnia through a picture hanging in his bedroom. The cousin went back later that year with a friend through a gate in the wall surrounding their school. Both times they had extended adventures in Narnia, but were back to England within minutes.

Some years later five of these children were killed in a railway accident—and all met together in Narnia.

Many of us were raised on these stories by C. S. Lewis[1]—or we raised our children on them. Lewis writes about what he calls two worlds: the fantasy world of Narnia, where most of the action of these stories takes place, and the real world of England, with bombing raids, boarding schools, "progressive" education, absent parents, and railway accidents. The background world of England is real enough—and dreary. It is in the fantasy world that our real-world experiences and emotions are exposed. Ultimately, the fantasy world is more real than the real world.

In Lewis's stories, the two worlds exist at the same time, but they follow different rules, including different notions of time, where a thousand years in one world can be as but a day in the other (2 Pet 3:8). They begin to remind us of the two worlds, or two kingdoms, that Christians claim: the kingdom of this world, and the kingdom of heaven. One crucial difference between experience in Lewis's worlds and the Christian experience of faith is that in Lewis's books, the children are either in one world or the other, but never in both at once. Yet we as Christians spend all our time physically in the kingdom of this world but as exiles from the kingdom of God. We are constantly in, or answerable to, both kingdoms.

This can be very uncomfortable,[2] as Ellul reminds us. We can, of course, deal with the discomfort by living according to the rules of the kingdom of this world, while still nominally claiming citizenship in the kingdom of heaven and membership in a church. For a while that may seem to work—until we realize that the church has taken on the characteristics of the world, and the world has disguised itself as the church. We must admit there can be no conflating the two kingdoms, and we must understand the differences between them.

Where can we be reminded of the differences? There is, first of all, the Bible. The writer of Psalm 119 speaks of being an "exile

1. Lewis, *Chronicles of Narnia.*
2. Ellul, *Presence,* 17.

... on earth" in verse 19. But an exile from where? From an idea? A goal? A promise? Was the writer just speaking poetically?

Nearly a thousand years later, Jesus proclaimed: "My kingdom is not of this world" (John 18:36). That Jesus was being tried because of his leadership in a kingdom suggests that those accusing him felt his kingdom was real enough to be a threat: hardly "merely" an idea or "just" a future promise. Jesus, shortly before in his farewell discourse in John 15, had explained to his disciples in some detail that the kingdom of this world would hate them precisely because they were not "of the world," did not belong to it (see v. 19).

When Peter wrote a few years later to Christians dispersed among various nations and living among foreigners, he reminded them that they were living "away from home" (1 Pet 1:1, 17), and urged them, as "visitors and pilgrims," to live holy lives (2:11; 1:16). We could assume Peter meant their "home" to be the land of Israel. However, the echoes from the writer of Psalm 119, as well as the sentiments of David at the end of Psalm 39 ("I am . . . a nomad like all my ancestors"), all suggest that Peter was referring to a home other than the land of Israel; likely the kingdom "not of this world" that Jesus spoke of.

We find these ideas developed more fully in the book of Hebrews. Chapter 11 begins with the assertion that faith is what connects us with "realities that at present remain unseen." Immediately following this there is a one-sentence explanation of creation: the world that we can see was created by the unseen God. In other words, the kingdom of this world that we know and inhabit was derived from the kingdom of heaven. That kingdom, far from being only an idea or a metaphor, is the source of our world; that kingdom is prior to, and as real as, the kingdom of this world.

But the writer of Hebrews goes far beyond simply affirming another kingdom than the one we see and inhabit. We find great detail about the exploits of a dozen Old Testament characters, and the theme that seems to underlie each of these stories is their bond with the kingdom not of this world. It is faith which makes that bond, leading many commentators to see this section as a discourse on faith. A close look reveals that is it also a discourse on the kingdom of heaven.

Abel somehow understood that kingdom more than Cain, and was able to offer the appropriate sacrifice based on that understanding. Enoch was so connected with that kingdom (he "walked with God") that God "took him"—to that kingdom.

Noah became aware of "something that had never been seen before"; yes, he became aware by faith, but *what* he became aware of, the coming flood, was a judgment of the kingdom of heaven on the kingdom of this world.

However, it is with Abraham that we get the clearest picture of the kingdom not of this world. He, called by God, left his home and traveled to the promised land where he lived as a foreigner. However, instead of planting a flag and claiming the land for his descendants, he lived in tents and "looked forward to a city founded, designed, and built by God" (Heb 11:10) He, and the others, recognized that they were "strangers and nomads on earth" (v. 13); they were searching for "their real homeland," "a better homeland, their heavenly homeland" (vv. 14–15)—clearly not the land of Israel.

This entire review of Old Testament characters in chapter 11 is bracketed by comments directed to the contemporaries of the writer of Hebrews, comments that bring the discussion right up to the time of those first reading this letter. In chapter 10, the readers are reminded that when they had previously suffered insults and violence, they had accepted this treatment "happily," "knowing that you owned something that was better and lasting" (vv. 34–35) What that "something" might be is described more fully in chapter 12. There, the writer tells the readers that they, as the church, have come to "the city of the living God" and are "citizen[s] of heaven" (vv. 22–23). And finally, they are told that this is an "unshakable kingdom" that they have been given possession of (v. 28). In other words, pilgrim "citizens of heaven" who live on earth are always aware of something "beyond"; citizens of this world deny there is anything beyond.

All these biblical passages about our spiritual home use political language: words such as "exile," "foreigner," "homeland," "city," "citizen," and most of all "kingdom." We might expect in a spiritual discourse words like "faith," "prayer," "sin," "grace," and "holy," and all of those words are there as well: the kingdom of heaven is still a spiritual kingdom. But what we sometimes gloss over or ignore or deny is that it is also a political kingdom. We live in one kingdom but are citizens of another, equally real kingdom.

## Signs of the Two Kingdoms

Beyond the Bible itself, nuns and monks can remind us of the difference between the kingdoms. They are "signs," they say, of (and to) the kingdom of heaven. They signify not by being sinless (none of us is) or by claiming forgiveness (all of us can). They are signs because of some choices they make about how they live, choices that bring into relief some differences between the kingdom of this world and the kingdom of heaven. Poverty, chastity, and obedience point to three decisive tenets of the kingdom of this world: money, sex, and independence. None of these tenets are prohibited in the Kingdom of Heaven, none are *sinful*. Nor are poverty, chastity, and obedience to a worldly master required for the kingdom of Heaven. Nuns and monks are not examples for us to follow; they by their choices are *signs* pointing us to kingdom values.

We cannot understand the differences between the two kingdoms by trying to decide which values or assumptions are sinful. *We* are sinful; as long as we live physically in the kingdom of this world, we can move toward the kingdom of heaven only asymptotically. Move, not abide. The only place it is safe to abide is in Christ.

The Bible records the long, sordid tale of the kingdom of heaven in conflict with the kingdom of this world, from before recorded history to the first generation of the Christian church. The characters and cultures change, but the table of contents is all in Genesis. From Adam and Eve's desire to know good *and* evil spring all the other chapters: Cain's revenge on the innocent Abel, the tower of Babel, righteous Abraham faced with the corporate sin of Sodom and Gomorrah, and the other stories of Genesis, all echo throughout Scripture.

The theme of the two kingdoms in conflict remains the same, but the details change because the world keeps finding new ways to sin. Would Abraham have been as upset with tax collectors as John the Baptist was? Would Moses have called the most righteous subgroup of Israel hypocrites, the way Jesus did to the Pharisees? And yet for tax collectors it was not collecting taxes that was the sin, but collecting too much. And for Pharisees it was not following the law that was the sin, but missing the point of the law.

Sin infects the normal processes and activities of our lives, much like viruses infect the normal cells of our bodies. These "processes and activities" are what William Stringfellow and others have identified as principalities and powers[3]—all parts of creation, and all fallen. It is vital that we consider these principalities and powers as we think about the kingdom of heaven and what masquerades as the kingdom of heaven in the kingdom of this world. More to the point, our subject here is modern biomedical health care and how to understand it in light of the two kingdoms. Modern medicine is very much one of these normal cells taken over by a virus, a principality.

But medicine is by no means the only principality. The principalities are legion, says Stringfellow: "they include all institutions, all ideologies, all images, all movements, all causes, all corporations, all bureaucracies, all traditions, all methods and routines, all conglomerates, all races, all nations, all idols"[4]—any structure or power, in fact, that can become autonomous from the kingdom of heaven. We mentioned earlier money, sex, and independence; they too are principalities. As examples, we will consider how two common principalities can become "infected" by the kingdom of this world: money (the principality that prompted nuns and monks to their vow of poverty) and communication (a much more contemporary example of infection).

3. Stringfellow, *An Ethic*, 77–106; Yoder, *Politics*, 144; Wink, *Powers*, 22–36.
4. Stringfellow, *An Ethic*, 78.

## Money

Some have said pride is the chief of the seven cardinal sins; money holds a similar role among the principalities. The Israelite prophets warned their people about the abuse of wealth, and Jesus' teachings continued in the same vein. The first beatitude extols its opposite (Matt 5:3), and Jesus says later that it is easier for a camel to go through the eye of a needle than for a rich person to enter heaven (Matt 19:24). Paul says that the love of money is the root of all evil (1 Tim 6:10), and defines adequate wealth as enough to buy only food and clothing (1 Tim 6:8). If anything, the New Testament warnings about wealth had become more stringent than even the most vituperative Old Testament prophet.

Early religious orders of the church adhered to voluntary poverty as one of their vows. Clearly the church had not conquered the temptations to wealth; there would be no need for the "sign" of poverty if it had. Two thousand years later we have still made no progress. There is very little difference between the world's understanding of wealth and the church's. The increasing split in world wealth between the rich and the poor is mirrored exactly in the church. In the kingdom of this world, that inequity is a scandal; in the kingdom of heaven it is iniquity (=inequity).

No great movement at the beginning of the twenty-first century seeks to redress this iniquity. The last great attempt—communism—failed, possibly because it was not a Christian program but a Christian heresy, claiming values of the kingdom of heaven without God. It failed too because people are sinful; capitalism succeeds (as an economic system, not a system to redress inequity) for precisely the same reason: people's sinful greed.

Not only has there been no recent outcry about rich Christians, but there is a resurgence of voices claiming allegiance to the kingdom of heaven who are openly siding with wealth. The argument seems to be that the wealth can be used to advance the kingdom of heaven; poor people either deserve their fate (the one who doesn't work shouldn't eat) or are objects of the charity of the rich. This view of wealth and poverty is the converse of the communist heresy: it names God without the values of the kingdom. Perhaps this is what it means to take the name of the Lord in vain.

## Communication

Script is as old as civilization; speech far older. The stories of our origins passed down orally in the Israelite community were finally written down and form the beginning of our Bible. Much of the rest of the Bible is the written record of what people said and did; at the end are some copies of letters they wrote. Script and speech communicated the gospel to Europe, and preserved it there for over a millennium. When the Renaissance unleashed science and technology, one of the first developments was the printing press, and the first book produced was the Bible. It would appear that we have finally found a development that really serves the kingdom of heaven.

Just as changes in transportation began slowly, so changes in communication proceeded slowly at first: photography, tele-graph, telephone, and radio in the nineteenth century, and film and television in the early twentieth. It wasn't until the late twen-tieth century, however, that the rate of change began to speed up. With computers, both the amount of information we could communicate, and the speed, increased dramatically—and hasn't yet stopped increasing. Computers only a few years old are "dino-saurs"; a letter crossing the country in two days is "snail mail." If it isn't instantaneous, it's too slow.

We have already identified the pattern: the kingdom of this world providing tools for the propagation of the kingdom of heaven. There are Christian radio and television networks, Chris-tian recording companies, Christian films, Christian magazines, Christian publishers, Christian politicians—and, as we have seen, Christian celebrities. Since effective marketing requires some recognition of cultural lowest common denominators, the media-presented kingdom of heaven cannot look very different from the kingdom of this world. At best, it is shallow; at worst, heresy. As the gospel becomes a product to sell quickly, we borrow the wisdom of advertising and condense it into slogans and sound-bites.

Even if we in the kingdom of heaven avoid the Christian media, we are infected with speed and efficiency. In the same way that money, sex, and power are all mixed up together, so too are transportation, management, and communication. We learned speed from jets and computers, and efficiency from management. We don't know what patience is anymore, even though it is the biblical trait. The efficiently managed media expose us to more than we can digest and encourage us to consume it all. We consume ideas and food and experiences and travel and gadgets—consume them all but have no time to digest them. We are the rich, well-fed, laughing, respected people that Luke's version of the Beatitudes said were woeful (Luke 6:24–25).

## Leaks: An Introduction

We could analyze race or sex or nations or universities or church denominations or any corporation or an "-ism" the same way. What we might find is how often the kingdom of this world masquerades as, or leaks into, our kingdom-of-heaven activities. But does the leak ever go the other way? Can the kingdom of heaven leak into the kingdom of this world? Can we even talk of a "good leak"? C. S. Lewis proposed in *Mere Christianity* the idea of the Christian faith as a "good infection," and this is the concept I am proposing: something small, like yeast or a seed or an infecting organism, that affects the whole of something else.[5] An odor, either foul or pleasant, can leak into a room and affect everyone there. Light does the same in a room, and salt in food. In using the idea of "leaks," I am suggesting nothing beyond the biblical yeast or salt or light.

Here is another cautionary comment: in talking of two kingdoms and of leaks between them, we can inadvertently come to think of them as two self-sufficient entities that can (or ought to)

---

5. See Lewis, *Mere Christianity*, book 4, chapter 4.

remain separate, like water pipes and sewage pipes—with a leak between them being disastrous. But this would be as inaccurate as considering the human soul and the human body as two self-sufficient entities. To change the metaphor, and to invoke Lewis once again, we are looking for the wardrobes, the places of connection between England and Narnia.

Just a cursory look at the biblical record uncovers innumerable stories of events that transcend the "rules" of the kingdom of this world, stories that suggest a breach in the barrier between the kingdoms, a Narnia experience. Sometimes that breaking through was for judgment: the flood in Noah's time, the confusion of languages at Babel, the destruction of Sodom and Gomorrah, the ten plagues on Egypt, several other plagues on the Israelites in the wilderness. But there were also times when the breach was for blessing: Sarah's pregnancy, the exodus from Egypt, the giving of the law, the stopping of the plagues on the Israelites.

However, as the Old Testament record continues, it seems that dramatic stories of the kingdom of heaven breaking through into the kingdom of this world gradually fade. The judgment of God on the Israelites, recorded in Kings, Chronicles, and the prophets, is portrayed as a consequence of their own behavior more than as a leak between the kingdoms. Large-scale reversals of plagues in Numbers give way to a few individual healings by Elijah and Elisha in Kings. There are certainly quite dramatic leaks in Daniel and Jonah, but they aren't leaks that change the course of history.

Then, the pattern changes in the New Testament. At first glance it appears that Jesus performs the same type of individual miracles Elijah and Elisha performed, only more of them. We have, for example, the record of only three healing miracles by Elijah and Elisha, but over two dozen by Jesus. The pattern change, however, is far more profound than just an increase in miracles. In the Gospels we find the entrance of the King of the kingdom of heaven into the kingdom of this world. This is Narnia's Aslan actually living in dreary England. It is the ultimate leak.

But consider how that leak happened: Since the kingdom of this world is corporal, and the kingdom of heaven and its King are spiritual (John 4:24), any leaking from the spiritual to the corporal will appear at least strange, and often frightening. Look at God announcing the law on Mount Sinai (Exod 20; Deut 5); look at Jesus casting demons out of a man and allowing them to enter a herd of pigs (Matt 8:28–34; Mark 5:1–20; Luke 8:26–39). We might expect the ultimate leak, then, to be even more strange, visible, and frightening. To be sure, when the leak first started the shepherds were "sore afraid," as was a king of this world (Herod), who saw a political threat in Jesus' birth. And of course the magi (the "three kings" of the Christmas carol) came to worship (see Matt 2; Luke 2).

Other than the above, no one else seems to have noticed. That's because the entrance of God into the world was incarnational: God took a corporal, carnal body: the one thing in this world which is not strange or frightening. If Aslan came to live in England, he would look like Oliver Twist, not an escaped circus lion.

A reasonable question follows: what has happened since then to miraculous leaks between the kingdoms? Beginning with the scientific revolution, we Christians have not been sure what to do about miracles reported after New Testament times. Are they tricks of perception? Wish fulfillments? Real miracles? The question bothers us, especially as members of some Christian denominations today regularly report healing miracles, and other Christians never see them. What's going on?

The question need not be troubling or threatening at all. Maybe there are miracles and always have been, but we don't know how to look for them anymore—they being below the radar of our scientific minds and tools. But on the other hand maybe that ultimate leak, the incarnation, is the ultimate miracle, and is happening all the time (under the radar), incarnationally, as we, the body of Christ, carry out the work of Christ. That work is called love. Maybe the ultimate leak is to "despiritualize" the leaks, to give them body.

However we see it, the ultimate leak, the incarnation, is profound, and gives the pattern for all of God's ongoing activity—and all of our ongoing participation in God's life on earth. As

Barbara Duden acknowledges, the incarnation is pivotal for Illich, the "prime mover" for everything we Christians do.[6]

## To Summarize

The Bible claims that there are two worlds, or two kingdoms: an earthly, physical one and a spiritual one. There is, further, evidence of what I'm calling leaks between the kingdoms: our experience in the kingdom of this world leaks into how we try to live spiritual lives, yet there is biblical evidence of the kingdom of heaven leaking into our world, most fully demonstrated in the incarnation.

We have also looked at some characteristics of our modern life, some principalities and powers (see Eph 6:12), and as each develops and grows in influence, we have identified a pattern: we celebrate the increasing power to do something and assume that what we do is in our control, and is good. However, the good we think we are doing does not always reflect the values of the kingdom of heaven. More than this, each of the forces, as it becomes more powerful, becomes both autonomous and apparently essential: each shows itself to be a fallen power. Instead of controlling this power, we are controlled by it.

This, unfortunately, is also the case with modern biomedical health care. What is troubling is that we have recognized this in health care less than in some of the other areas just described. When I first thought and wrote about these principalities, I did not include medicine among them—an irony all the more striking since I am a medical doctor. My, and our, inability to see the disconnect between modern medicine and the values of the kingdom arises partly because the subject matter of medicine is life and death, with medicine offering what we all want: to improve and prolong life and to avoid and defeat death. Before examining in detail the gaps between modern medical care and biblical healing, then, we need to look carefully at death and life.

6. Duden, "Ivan Illich."

# Chapter 2

# Death and Life

DEATH AND LIFE ARE, for most of us, words with obvious meanings; we don't see the need for definitions. In fact, dictionaries don't always help that much, sometimes defining one as the opposite of the other. But our lack of precise definitions doesn't bother most of us. In both medicine and theology, these words describe the atmosphere in which we work: the playing field, the subject matter, the boundaries. The same is true for laypeople generally. We all know what being alive is, and we all know what being dead is. And we mostly agree that being alive is better than being dead—unless what is alive is a pathogenic bacteria or a demon or a growing cancer or self-will.

More important, however, than precisely defining *death* and *life* is recognizing that doctors and theologians may assume very different meanings when they use these words. The playing fields of biomedical health care and spirituality may overlap, but the boundaries are different. Nevertheless, an undisputed goal in both health care and spirituality, as well as for the general public, is life; a generally agreed foe is death. But what do each of us mean by these words?

## Definitions

We will begin with biomedical definitions because they are clear. Life is when the heart is beating and the lungs breathing; death is when they aren't. The precise definition of life can be fine-tuned with discussions of temporary cessations of cardiac and respiratory activity (when on a heart-lung machine or during a cardiac arrest) or measurement of brain waves, but the fundamental definition is biological: *life* means biological life. That is the reason for the term *biomedical*—medicine that sustains or improves biological life. Throughout this book I use the prefix *bio-* (*biomedicine, bio-mechanisms, bio-life, bio-death*) to clarify when I am using these biological definitions. *Bioethics* is ethical reflection on how we engage with these biological processes.

Spiritual definitions do not have this same focus on biological life. In the Genesis creation story, for example, life (plant life) is created on the third day with no fanfare, sandwiched between the separation of waters on the second day and the creation of the sun and moon on the fourth (see Gen 1:6–20).

The first time a form of the word *life* is used in Genesis is with fish on the fifth day. Human and animal life are both created on the next day, but human life at least has the distinction of being created in God's image (Gen 1:26–27). Death doesn't appear until the next chapter; it is not the opposite of fish or animal or human life, but the threatened result of eating from the tree of the knowledge of good and evil (Gen 2:16).

For biomedicine, then, life is protoplasmic activity; death its cessation or absence. For spirituality, death is independence from or disobeying God; life is the opposite. But that is only the beginning of the spiritual understanding. Spiritual death, unlike biological death, is not necessarily a permanent condition. There even appears to be movement back and forth between spiritual death and spiritual life, and that is irrespective of biological life; a person, for example, can be physically dead but spiritually alive. In addition, biological life always precedes biological death; but since the fall, spiritual death always precedes spiritual life (Rom 5–8).

Saint John (in 1 John 3;13–14) even connects this movement from death to life with the two kingdoms: being hated by this world coincides with this death-to-life movement.

Because of this fluid understanding, life and death in spiritual language are sometimes used as code words, representing life and death not as final states but as directions. Adam and Eve did not immediately die when they ate the fruit of the tree of knowledge of good and evil; they *began* to die. When Jesus offers "eternal life," those receiving it must understand it as the *beginning* of that life.

Using the language of the last chapter, the kingdom of this world is the locus for biological life and death; the kingdom of heaven is the locus for spiritual death and life. Unfortunately this only makes clear how different the two sets of definitions are. It is almost as if we need different sets of words.

But we still use the same words—*life* and *death*—for both spiritual and biological life and death. The confusion that occurs, though, is not so much within medicine or theology but in common speech. The general public accepts a mostly biological definition for these words but carries them with spiritual connotations. Life becomes not just protoplasmic activity but something sacred; death is not just cessation of protoplasmic activity but on some level separation from God. When I want to make the difference clear, I call biological life "bio-life" and spiritual life "Life."

## Idolatry

To further understand how—and how much—we honor life and death in the kingdom of this world, we need to look briefly again at *where* that kingdom is in order consider idolatry in it. In the Preface we suggested that biblically *Babylon* is a code word for the kingdom of this world and all of its manifestations. Nazi Germany was a Babylon; America at times has shown itself to be a Babylon. According to Jacques Ellul, both the United States and the Soviet Union, despite vastly different economic and political foundations, equally depended on rational, efficient techniques in the control of their societies.[1] Today, all modern societies are "technocracies" or "technopolies," modern labels for today's Babylons. The pride and materialism of Babylon in Revelation 17 and 18 are pictures, not only of America, but of any modern society. And with materialism comes idolatry.

The word *idol* comes from the Greek *eidolōn*, which means "image." Images—such as photographs of family members who live far away—remind us of what or who we cannot see. But sometimes the route from making an image of something we honor and respect to worshiping the image itself is a short route. The second commandment therefore prohibited "graven images," or idols, precisely for this reason: Israelites were instructed not only to refrain from *making* the images but also (and especially) from worshiping and serving them (Exod 20:4–6; Deut 5:8–10). The essence of idolatry is not image-making but image-worship. By the time of the New Testament, an image was no longer necessary for idolatry: Col 3:5 describes greed and other similar attitudes and behaviors as idols. Meanwhile, the neutral concept of image had come to be associated with a different Greek word, *eikōn* ("icon"), used to denote both Christ as the image of God, and the image of the beast in Rev 13.

Idolatry, then, is serving or giving ultimate worth (worthship = worship) to something other than God; an idol is a false god. Most idols in America—or in any Babylon—today, while they may have images associated with them, are ideologies or institutions or behaviors; they can be the principalities examined in the previous chapter—or any other principality or power. But preeminent among them all are death and life.

This idolatry of death and life can be, frankly, difficult to grasp. We can more easily understand giving ultimate worth to and serving, say, the entertainment industry or materialism or our job or computer technology or capitalism—though we can usually see the idolatry of others better than our own misplaced worship. Christians can even idolize the Bible or the church, giving ultimate worth to them instead of God—a difficult but important

1. Ellul, *Technological Society*, xxv–xxvi.

18

distinction to make. But we usually end up idolizing what we naturally like, and that is why it is so difficult to understand what is meant by idolizing death.

## Death

Yet the claim of William Stringfellow throughout *An Ethic for Christians and Other Aliens in a Strange Land* is precisely that. He speaks not only of the "power of death" and of "death reigning" in America, but also of the "idolatry of death," saying death is the "preemptive idol," "the idol of the idols."[2] Then in his introduction to the 1967 American edition of Jacques Ellul's foundational book *The Presence of the Kingdom*, Stringfellow speaks of "the power of death as the ruler of this world," and again of the "idolatry of death."[3] Indeed Ellul himself in the first chapter of the book says "The will of the world is always a will to death, a will to suicide."[4] What does all this mean?

Stringfellow's own explanations refer to wars and genocides but also to government or industrial policies that dehumanize people. Clearly he is using more of a spiritual definition of *death*, but one that could include bio-death. *Death* for him is a code word for anything that hurts or isolates or abandons or dehumanizes people. These actions and policies are the *beginnings* of death; continued, they would lead to bio-death. Understood this way, Stringfellow and Ellul's claims become more clear.

First, the ultimate power of any state is literally to bring about death: the authority to arm police with lethal weapons, to recruit and deploy the military, and—in America at least—the ability to impose the death penalty on those convicted of capital crimes. The state does not have equivalent power or authority to produce or create life—only to "protect" it. In addition, industry and the state together permit and sponsor innumerable death-dealing

2. Stringfellow, *An Ethic*, 68, 70, 126.

3. Stringfellow, "Introduction," 3–4.

4. Ellul, *Presence*, 28.

activities, producing and permitting vehicles that annually kill tens of thousands of people, advertising a lifestyle that involves consuming animal fat and engaging in long periods of inactivity—both of which lead to fatal diseases; allowing environmental destruction and nuclear weapons, both of which could ultimately make the planet uninhabitable. And of course there is iatrogenic disease—disease caused by medical care itself. The list is far longer. In most of these, death—real, bio-death—is but a "side effect" of our technology or our choices.

Why is it that we accept so many activities in our culture that dependably kill people? Or the other activities that just lead to the *beginnings* of death: occult and open racism, increasing economic inequity, producing and consuming waste, mindless entertainment, utter lack of job security . . . another endless list. None of us *like* death, and most of the time we do not consciously choose death.

But if the connection between so many of our everyday activities and death is so clear, why do we continue to live this way? It appears that Ellul is correct: "The will of the world is always a will to death, a will to suicide."[5] Stringfellow just goes one step further: if we continuously choose activities that lead to death, we are serving those activities and granting them ultimate worth. Those activities, and the death common to all of them, must be our idol.

## Life

If it is true, then, that in our culture we functionally worship death, it initially seems strange that another disciple of Ellul, Ivan Illich, would declare life itself to be an idol. Yet twenty years after *Medical Nemesis* he wrote, "'A life' is the most powerful idol the church has had to face in the course of its history."[6] Is Illich contradicting Stringfellow, or are both life and death idols for us? How?

5. Ellul, *Presence*, 28.
6. Illich, *Brave New Biocracy*.

To understand, we need first to return to the definitions we started with. Stringfellow and Ellul are using mostly spiritual definitions for death; Illich seems to be using more of a biomedical definition for the life we idolize (he calls it "a life"). But how he, and we, arrive at this definition is the key to understanding what Illich means by life as an idol.

Throughout most of history, there was no clear distinction between spiritual life and biomedical life. Nature itself was alive. In Genesis 1, the *earth* produced vegetation and animals; in Psalm 148, all parts of nature—sun, moon, stars, weather, mountains, plants, animals, people, angels—were to praise God. There was no problem with "inert" earth *producing* something, with "inert" stars or mountains praising God.

The "birthing power of nature was rooted in the world's being contingent on the incessant creative will of God." The very existence of the world depended on the "graceful sharing" of God's own life.[7] In medieval Europe there was no distinction between spiritual life and bio-life because there was no concept of biological life. All nature, whether animate or inanimate, was contingent on the life of God; all nature was alive.

Science changed that. The wonder of the science of the nineteenth century was that it discovered *how* things work; it uncovered mechanisms, both in the natural world and in the human body. Applying what we know about how the body works is the foundation for all of the successful treatments of biomedicine.

This science by itself does not cause us to idolize life, but it does tempt us to see human life as *not* contingent on God 's own life being shared with us. If we understand, for example, that seeds placed in the earth, watered, and given sunlight will produce plants, we don't speak of the earth itself, or God, producing the plants; the seeds do, by a "natural" process. When we comprehend nutrition and oxygenation, we can explain how they keep the brain and heart functioning. We no longer assume human life is contingent on God's life because we understand life more proximally to be dependent on nutrition and oxygenation. This proximate

7. Illich, *Brave New Biocracy.*

contingency—on food and air—is so satisfying that it keeps us from thinking about more ultimate contingencies. Eventually we let them go. Life has become autonomous bio-life, separate from God.

It is this life that Illich says we venerate, apart from God; this is the life which has become for us an idol. But look: in Genesis 2, death was at root separation from God. Yet we just saw that autonomous bio-life is also separation from God. The idolatry of death that Ellul and Stringfellow speak of, and the idolatry of life that Illich speaks about, appear to be the very same thing. The difference is in the context in which we usually use these words "life" and "death." Stringfellow often speaks of the idolatry of death in a political context; Illich refers to the idolatry of life in a clinical context.

Following this general division, we will in this book look at biblical stories of healing in two groups: those that raise questions of power, and that are therefore ultimately political (Part 2), and those look at the nature of healing, and that are more clinical (Part 3). In the Conclusion (Part 4) we will revisit several of the book's themes as they are revealed metaphorically in the healing miracles, and finally come back to the theme of this chapter with a look at resurrection.

# *Part Two*

## Political: Power over Death

"The ancient teachers of this science [alchemy]," said he, "promised impossibilities and performed nothing. The modern masters promise very little; they know that metals cannot be transmuted and that the elixir of life is a chimera. But these philosophers, whose hands seem only made to dabble in dirt, and their eyes to pore over the microscope or crucible, have indeed performed miracles. They penetrate into the recesses of nature and show how she works in her hiding places. They ascend into the heavens; they have discovered how the blood circulates, and the nature of the air we breathe. They have acquired new and almost unlimited powers . . ."

—MARY W. SHELLEY, *FRANKENSTEIN*, 1818

The monster: "Remember that thou hast made me more powerful than thyself . . . You are my creator, but I am your master."

—MARY W. SHELLEY, *FRANKENSTEIN*, 1818

# 3

# Demons

## *The Power of Medicine and the Power of God*

THE FIRST RECORDED HEALING miracle of Jesus bears close scrutiny. After his baptism by John in the Jordan River (Luke 3:21–22), and after the temptation ordeal by the devil in the wilderness (Luke 4:1–12), Jesus goes back home to Galilee. His opening speech is dramatic enough: he reads from Isaiah about good news to the poor, liberty to captives, sight to the blind, freedom to the downtrodden—and then proclaims in the synagogue of his hometown, Nazareth, that he is the fulfillment of the Isaiah passage (Luke 4:16–21; see Isa 61:1–3).

Not surprisingly, no one believes him. He goes on to compare these unbelieving neighbors of his to the Israelites in the days of Elijah, when benefits seem to be directed at non-Israelites. Then they try to kill him (Luke 4:23–30).

Another Sabbath, it may have been the next week, he was teaching in the lakeside town of Capernaum, his new home. Listeners noted a quality in his teaching they were apparently not used to; the Gospel writers simply call it "authority" (Matt 7:29; Mark 1:27; Luke 4:36) What happens next made clear what this "authority" is. A man in the synagogue shouts, "I know who you are: the Holy One of God!" (Mark 1:24; Luke 4:34). He is confirming Jesus' claim to be fulfilling the Isaiah prophecy, and he is explaining the source of Jesus' "authority." Jesus, he is announcing, is not just another good teacher, but has a special relationship with God. He comes just short of declaring him the expected Messiah.

How did he know? It is at this point that the story becomes strange—at least to modern ears—because the Gospel writers say that the man had an unclean spirit or demon. Jesus knew this immediately, told the demon to be quiet, and commanded it to leave the man. It did, causing the man to have a convulsion in the process. The people in the synagogue readily accepted that something powerful and good had happened, and Jesus' reputation spread rapidly (Mark 1:21–28; Luke 4:31–37).

Shortly after telling this story, both Mark and Luke confirm that it is not an isolated incident. Luke 4:41 says other demons declared Jesus to be the Son of God and knew he was the Christ, the expected Messiah, and Mark 1:34 says simply that the demons knew who he was. Later on, when Jesus casts the demons called Legion out of a man and into a herd of pigs, and two thousand demon-possessed pigs race into a lake and drown themselves (Matt 8:28–34; Mark 5:1–20; Luke 8:26–39), the story is the same. Those demons also know who Jesus is, and they shout his name—the son of the Most High God (Matt 8:29; Mark 5:7; Luke 8:28).

However, before being cast out of that man (or men—Matthew says there are two), the demons cause rather different symptoms than with the first fellow, who only shouts and convulses. This man with the legion of demons seems absolutely psychotic, violent, and self-destructive—as well as antisocial! He also is cured after the demons are cast out, and is found clothed and in his right mind.

Unfortunately, the significance of these exorcisms (to which we will return shortly) can be lost today, especially by people raised under biomedicine. We want to know what the Bible means by "demons" and "unclean spirits"; even more we want to know what diagnoses these possessed people had. Did the first "really" have epilepsy, the second schizophrenia? There is another apparent epileptic said to have a demon, and three Gospel writers tell us that the disciples cannot cast out this demon. There is some detail about his affliction, and it sounds very much like a seizure disorder (Mark 9:17–24; Luke 9:37–43). So is *demon* a biblical code word for disorders in which people behave strangely, as psychotics and epileptics do?

Then there are those who were said to be demon-possessed and couldn't talk—mutism being, I suppose, another form of strange behavior (Matt 9:32–33, 12:22, 15:30; Mark 7:37; Luke 11:14). Most of the time the Gospel writers call these people demon-possessed as well. Matthew tells of two different mute people who had demons (9:32; 12:22–24), and Luke (11:14) records the story of the one that earned Jesus the reputation of casting out demons using the power of the prince of demons, Beelzebub. And when Mark (9:14–29) tells the story of the epileptic the disciples couldn't handle, he says that the man had a deaf and dumb unclean spirit. But Mark tells of another man (7:31–37), deaf and with a speech impediment, and mentions no demon. Just to complicate things further, the Greek word involved in these passages, *kōphos*, is sometimes translated as "dumb" or "mute," and other times as "deaf"—and it actually means "dull" or "blunt."

I have a reason for this brief, confusing foray into biblical classification of disease: to illustrate the difficulty of superimposing our biomedical taxonomy of disease onto the biblical record. Trying to understand one using the terminology of the other is like trying to describe tropical rainy and dry seasons with the terminology of temperate summer and winter. Or trying to use the concepts of the kingdom of this world to understand the kingdom of heaven. They don't fit. As with the definitions of *death* and *life* in chapter 2, there are spiritual and biomedical categories, and while they may overlap, they are not the same. John's statement at the end of his Gospel (20:30–31) probably would apply to the other Gospel writers as well: they were writing devotional records—certainly accurate ones (Luke 1:1–4), but neither intended nor able to be biomedical records.

27

But the disconnect between the categories is not complete; the subject matter—people who are ill—is the same for spiritual and biomedical writers. Since it is only the classification that differs, there are reasons to not even try to overlay one on the other. We need to take the biblical story on its own terms, reading to understand what the writers were trying to convey.

## Returning Then to Demons

It is no accident that the first recorded healing miracle of Jesus is an exorcism, or that a demon identified him—a representative from the spiritual world identifying another representative from the spiritual world ("takes one to know one"). The origin of Jesus' healing power is that he is the Son of God, the Christ. The same message is clear from the events surrounding the casting out of the demon from the epileptic boy. All three Synoptic Gospel writers record this sequence: First there is the Transfiguration, where Jesus is revealed to his close friends as the Beloved Son of God, the Chosen One. Then there is the demon that the disciples cannot cast out, and following this is Jesus' prophecy that he will be killed and raised to life again.

The bookends of the healing event proclaim Jesus' identity: the Son of God, the One who saves by his death. But the event itself this time is not another demon announcing Jesus' identity, but a poignant tale of human smallness. The disciples can't cast this demon out, and Jesus, instead of encouraging them, simply says they are part of a faithless or unbelieving generation. Desperate for help, the boy's father pleads with Jesus to do something "if you can," and Jesus tells him that of course he can—if the man has faith. Rushing headlong into the gentle word trap Jesus had set up, the man says, "I believe!"—and then, as if suddenly realizing that he too is part of the unbelieving generation, "Help my unbelief!" (Mark 9:22–24 RSV). Jesus apparently does, and casts out the demon, one who never does name him. But the event itself named him—as the one who could do what the disciples could not.

## Jesus' Power versus Biomedicine's Power

It is, then, Jesus tangling with demons that establishes not only his identity but also the source of his power. The demons say it: He is the Son of the Most High God. His power is contingent on this relationship with God. After healing the man who had been lame for thirty-eight years at the pool of Bethzatha (John 5:1–9), Jesus gives a speech that makes this clear (John 5:17–18). He does nothing alone; whatever he does is because of his relationship with the Father and through the power of the Father. His healing is *contingent* on God.

Compare this, now, to the power of biomedical healing. Biomedical technology is contingent only on science: the activity of people over the last several centuries to uncover the mechanisms of nature. But, as we saw in chapter 2, the work of science has gradually become autonomous from the life of God. There is nothing in science itself that proscribes a spiritual understanding of life. Science, and especially its offspring technology, looks only at mechanisms and how to modify them. The problem enters when we equate the mechanisms of life (which we have the power to modify) with Life itself; when Life that was historically contingent on God, or at least on nature, becomes autonomous from God and nature; when Life becomes reduced to bio-life only—what Illich called "a life."

We don't have to make this reduction—I say this as a doctor. But we have—perhaps not each of us individually, but the entire system that teaches and sustains us—limited the subject matter of health care to bio-life. Bio-ethics accepts this limitation, allowing the biomedical definition of life to supplant a broader, spiritual definition of Life. In the name of respecting the autonomy of people who no longer think spiritually, bio-ethics concurred. We, biomedicine, are autonomous from God; mirroring this autonomy, the first pillar of Western bio-ethics is the autonomy of every patient. And we not only recognize this autonomy, we celebrate it.

More than this, our system of biomedicine reigns. There are plenty of other systems competing with ours, claiming to heal: all of the members of complementary and alternative medicine, all of the healing religions, all of the self-care advocates. Many are popular, but none can produce the same results so consistently as biomedicine; none has the same power—at least regarding measurable change in bio-mechanisms. The hegemony of biomedicine is a direct result of its power.

But if biomedicine works, what is the problem with letting it reign? There are several.

First, biomedicine is very effective, or "productive," but it is also highly counterproductive; this is the thesis of Illich's *Medical Nemesis*. This counterproductivity is, in fact, a direct result of its power. Powerful medical technology certainly injures people "accidentally" (iatrogenic disease); recently there has been much discussion about the claim that one hundred thousand Americans die every year as a result of "medical errors." This number is two or three times higher if we add in deaths from "side effects" of our medical technology not due to errors.[1] But as troubling as this is, it is not biomedicine's most significant counterproductivity. "Medicalization of life" is, by medicalizing all of life, we narrow our focus to how medical technology can improve life, and in doing so diminish historical, cultural, and spiritual ways of healing.

Second, power alone is not a reason to do something. We may have the power for interplanetary space travel, but that does not mean we must engage in it. We may have the power to change the shape of someone's nose, or determine the sex of their child before birth, but that power is not a mandate to do so. Acting only according to the availability of technology is called the technological imperative. It is, of course, a false imperative.

Third, the approaches, especially the use statistics and probability, necessary for applying biomedical advances to an entire population can "disembody" us. We will consider this difficult concept more fully in chapter 5.

Finally, whether it had to be this way or not, the power of biomedicine is accompanied by autonomy from God and nature, and the result is a narrowed focus on mechanisms only. Though

1. Starfield, "Is US Health."

the reign of biomedicine has become worldwide, the reductionism that accompanies it is very recent in history (emerging only since the scientific revolution of the sixteenth and seventeenth centuries) and almost unknown outside of Western thought. I recognize this reductionism especially when I practice in Africa.

The norm, historically and geographically, has been to see our lives as part of something else, something bigger—something spiritual. Outside of biomedicine, people perceive metaphorically (see Chapter 9). We even have remnants left in our speech: We say "I see what you mean" even though in that sentence we don't mean seeing with our eyes. We cannot let the reign of biomedicine go unchecked if its approach ignores the wisdom of the world throughout the ages.

## The Cosmos and Healing

It is worth pursuing this last point: Were people in other times and places wrong in their assumption that we are all part of something bigger? Or is our narrow, biomedical focus keeping us from seeing what people in other cultures still know? If the rest of the world is right, the fallout for our focused biomedical approach is enormous, because I can never be or remain ill apart from negative spin-offs in the cosmos of which I am part; I cannot be healed apart from beneficial spin-offs in the cosmos.

To a biomedical doctor, this may sound like New Age fluff, overblown language that means nothing because it cannot be measured. To an ecologist or a nurse, however, the concepts are obvious: if I am sick, my family may worry, there will be medical bills, and the tasks I had planned will be postponed or left undone. How far will the ripples spread? I may claim to be autonomous, but I cannot be autonomously ill. For the same reason, I cannot be autonomously healed.

The biblical healing miracles point in the same direction. Jesus claimed that his power, and by implication all healing power, is from God. The demons make this clear at Jesus' very first healing miracle. The story of the healing of the man born blind in John 9

(vv. 1–41) develops this same theme. The disciples are convinced that there is some sin underneath this affliction (see chapter 6 of this book) and simply want to clarify whether the sin is the man's or his parents' (v. 2). There was apparently a commonly held understanding that sin was somehow involved with his blindness, because later on the Pharisees revile him for being wholly (*holos*)—utterly, entirely—steeped in sin since birth (v. 34).

Jesus' answer to the disciples takes the discussion to a completely different level. He rejects the entire notion of blame for the blind man's condition, and in doing so links the yet-to-be-performed healing with the entire cosmos: says Jesus, the man was born blind so that the works of God might be displayed, or manifest, in him (v. 3). This man's healing is to be the conduit of God's power, offered and available to anyone who witnessed this power. The cosmos is about to be affected by the healing of one man.

But the story doesn't play out that way. The neighbors can't believe their eyes; the Pharisees at first doubt that any healing occurred, and if it did are scandalized that it took place on the Sabbath; and the Jews generally—beginning with the assumption that Jesus is a sinner—essentially accuse the healed man of being healed wrongly. Good evidence ("once I was blind but now I see" [vv. 9–11, 15]) is overridden by improper technique (healing on the Sabbath [v. 16]). Extraordinary power ("Ever since the world began it is unheard of for anyone to open the eyes of a man who was born blind" [v. 32]) is an extraordinary threat.

## To Summarize

What I have tried to show so far is this: Healing in the New Testament is by the power of Jesus, the Son of God. Healing in biomedicine is by the power of technology, the son of science. There is nothing inherent in science, an investigation of mechanisms, that insists we healers look only at mechanisms. But science itself only looks at mechanisms—and by doing so chooses to be independent from God. Bioethics (secular bioethics, at least), in order to help guide us in the use of the power of science for healing, must assume the same independence from God, and enshrines this in its first principle of autonomy.

So we have contingent power, dependent on God, and autonomous power, self-reliant. As we saw in the last miracle, extraordinary power, even the power to do good, is not automatically accepted by the ruling power; every power will consider a different power to be a threat. We have just introduced the next chapter.

# Chapter 4

# "Tell No One"

## The Power of Medicine vs. the Power of God

EARLY ON IN JESUS' public life, he tells the one he had just healed not to let anyone know about the healing (Mark 1:40–45). But he doesn't just *tell* him; he admonishes him sternly, and the Greek word Mark uses for *admonish* also means "to be moved with anger." The disease was leprosy, the healing was instantaneous, and the final instructions to the healed man were to show himself to the priest to confirm the healing and be let back into the community in accordance with the Jewish law—see Lev 13–14. So why does Jesus order the man to hide his healing from everyone except the priest?

Despite Jesus' stern admonition, the man tells everyone he runs into about his healing, and they all flock to Jesus with their needs—so many that Jesus cannot publicly enter the towns anymore. It is tempting to connect the order to "tell no one" with the crowded, chaotic situation that ensued when everyone knew, and to assume that Jesus wants to reduce his popularity and the resulting chaos. But he doesn't shun the popularity: at the feeding of the five thousand the disciples were dismayed at the sight of the crowd that follows them, and want them sent away; Jesus insists on teaching them, healing many of them, and feeding all of them, miraculously (Mark 6:30–44). A miracle of that size cannot be kept quiet.

While he is still in Galilee, we find the interwoven healings of the woman with the hemorrhage and the daughter of Jairus (Mark 5:21–43). This twelve year-old girl has died, and after raising her to life, Jesus tells the family not to tell anyone about it. But he doesn't just "tell" them; Mark says he charged them expressly (v. 43). Luke, in his telling of both this healing and the one noted above, says that Jesus ordered those involved not to tell anyone, and the Greek word for "order" means to transmit a message (Luke 8:43–56). But in the New Testament, this word is always used by people in authority: Jesus in the Gospels, civil authorities in Acts, and Paul in the Epistles. Nevertheless, Matthew tells us, the news of the girl's coming to life again spread everywhere (9:26).

Just after Matthew reports this, he tells the story of two blind men to whom Jesus gives sight by touching their eyes (9:27–31). Jesus admonishes them *sternly* (the same word Mark uses with Jesus' order to the leper) to tell no one, but they too spread the news everywhere. And in Mark there is a story of Jesus traveling outside of Galilee, to Decapolis, and finding a deaf man with a speech impediment. Jesus takes him aside to a private place away from the crowd (to avoid drawing attention to the healing?), touches his ears and tongue, heals him, then charges him expressly to tell no one. The man promptly proclaims what had happened to him (Mark 7:31–37).

Four times Jesus, with some intensity, orders people to tell no one about their healing, and each time they immediately disobey. Here is indeed an odd situation: a strict order of silence given from an authority, for no obvious reason, to people who have been healed, who immediately disobey the order, and face no apparent consequences. Beyond these four, there are other times that Jesus cautions silence with no reason given. Clearly there is a pattern here that is worth considering.

## Political Meaning of Jesus' Healings

William Stringfellow suggests that the orders to tell no one bespeak the political significance of Jesus' healings, a significance that becomes clear with the raising of Lazarus from death.[1] The implication seems to be that if those he heals are less public about the healings, Jesus will get in political trouble less quickly. We will look carefully at the Lazarus story to see what Stringfellow means, and work backward toward the other healings.

The story of the raising of Lazarus is only in the Gospel of John (chapter 11). There are but four miraculous healings recorded there, yet three are told in great detail, the healing of Lazarus being the last. It is in some of those details that we can see the political nature of this healing. When Jesus is first summonsed to Bethany to attend Lazarus in his illness, he declares the reason for that illness: to reveal the glory of God—which is somewhat parallel to the reason for the man being born blind two chapters earlier. That illness would have a "reason" at all is clearly a step beyond the biomedical understanding of disease as mechanism only. And in this case the reason, the glory of God, is a direct political threat.

The disciples are aware of this threat long before they know how Lazarus will be healed. They are with Jesus on the other side of the Jordan River where all of them had fled not long before to escape the threat of Jesus being stoned for blasphemy in Jerusalem (see John 10:31–39). Naturally they challenge Jesus' decision to return to Judea since the threat of being stoned is still there (11:7–8). Falsely claiming to be the Son of God—what Jesus was accused of—was a religious offense; *being* the Son of God was clearly a political offense, challenging the power structure in Jerusalem. The disciples know the risk; Thomas declares that they should accompany Jesus and accept the consequence: death (11:16).

It is, by the way, in the middle of this place of threatened and real bio-death where Ivan Illich finds the essence of Life. Here Jesus declares to Martha that he *is* Life—not the bio-life which Illich calls an idol and blasphemy, the life that biomedicine feels a responsibility for, that science has reduced to respiration and cardiac activity, that is for Illich just an immune system of feedback loops that keeps itself going. No, the Life that Jesus speaks of, and the

---

1. Stringfellow, *An Ethic*, 148–9; Stringfellow, *Instead*, 8.

Illich directs our attention to, is Life, contingent on God: Life that supersedes bio-death and conquers spiritual death.[2]

Just after the raising of Lazarus, the religious authorities in Jerusalem call a meeting. They are worried about the effects of Jesus' increasing popularity, not only on their own power, but also on their ethnicity (*ethnos*), their nation. If large numbers of people follow Jesus, they reason, they will neglect Jewish customs; the Imperial authority, Rome, would then have no reason to respect their nation, and would destroy them. Their conclusion is clear: they had better kill Jesus instead—but this time it is not because of the religious reason of blasphemy, but because of the political reason that his activity is a threat to their nation (see John 11:47–53).

Not long after this, Jesus is back in Bethany, once again with his friends Mary, Martha, and Lazarus. Mary, at least, knows he is soon to die, and anoints him with expensive ointment in preparation for his burial (John 12:3). A lot of people show up when they hear he is around, wanting to see not only him, but also Lazarus, the tangible evidence of his healing power. Those in authority, well aware of these events, see power slipping out of their hands, and feel they needed to be more proactive in controlling the situation. So, to destroy the evidence of Jesus' life-giving power, they decide to kill Lazarus as well (vv. 9–11). The political nature of their predicament is literally out in the open the next day when Jesus rides a donkey into Jerusalem, and people proclaim him the king of Israel (vv. 12–13). According to John, it is the raising of Lazarus that precipitates their praise and exaltation of Jesus (v. 17).

That Jesus' repeated instructions prohibiting those he healed from telling anyone are for political reasons is difficult to prove. But there can be no doubt about the political nature of Jesus' healings. The healings, especially that of Lazarus, show clearly the kind of power that Jesus had. Even though it is power to do good, the authorities are threatened. But the story of Lazarus shows to what lengths they will go to preserve their power: they are prepared to (and according to some church traditions did) kill Lazarus. When Jesus repeatedly orders those he healed to stay quiet about it, could

2. Illich, *Brave New Biocracy*.

one reason have been that he was trying to protect, not his own reputation, but their own lives?

## Political Meaning of Biomedical Healing

Now compare the political significance of Jesus' healing with the political significance of biomedical healing. Jesus knows early on that his healings will attract attention—unwanted attention—and it seems that he tries to reduce that attention by ordering those healed to be discreet. But note: the effectiveness of his healings is not in dispute. The authorities do not doubt that Lazarus came to life again. They try, quite unsuccessfully, to make a case that the man Jesus gave sight to was not the man born blind. They cannot deny the "medical" power of his healing; what they are determined to deny him is the "political" power that would grow out of this. If he really could heal, people would grant Jesus the authority to explain why things happened, or the power to name what was going on.

This is precisely the level at which we need to look at the power of biomedicine. It is undoubtedly power to modify the mechanics of bio-life, power to cure, and even at times power to heal, to make whole. That cannot be disputed. But the political power of biomedicine—the permission people delegate to biomedical providers to set society's healing agenda and to determine what we all need to maintain life and remain healthy—that is the power we need to address. That is the power to name what is going on, to be the savior, and to control people, the power that Father Katongole spoke of in the Preface.

To explore this, let us go back to the origins of biomedicine, in the middle of the nineteenth century before the germ theory of disease was widely accepted. There were several competing theories of disease among those in the medical power structure, with the definitive studies proving microorganisms yet to come. In 1848 Dr. Ignaz Semmelweis, by using antiseptic methods during birthing, was able to reduce deaths from postdelivery infection fifteen fold. But instead of being honored, he was dismissed and ostracized by his colleagues for the implicit assumption behind his method—that doctors (none of whom practiced antisepsis) were the reason for the previous high mortality.[3] It was not just ideas that got him in trouble; it was the power of his antiseptic method—which ended up implicating doctors. Those in power are more concerned about the political power to name what is going on than the medical power to heal.

We can see another slant to this matter of naming what is going on from a more recent example. In July 2000 the first International AIDS conference to be held on the African continent opened in Durban, South Africa, and South African president Thabo Mbeki gave the keynote address. In this address he said that the context in which AIDS flourished in Africa was poverty. Because of some previous debates he had been involved in, many at the conference and in the media interpreted Mbeki's speech as saying that poverty, *and not HIV*, caused AIDS—but even a superficial reading of the speech shows that he never denied the HIV causation. Biomedical scientists and the media following them assumed they had the right to name what was going on: that a virus alone causes AIDS. Mbeki was proposing another way to name what was going on, but the biomedical power structure was not willing to let go their monopoly on describing disease causation. Mbeki, like Semmelweis, was ostracized.

## The Power to Name

In the next chapter we will consider whether or not the power to heal automatically confers the power to name what is going on. But before doing so, it is worth exploring in some detail what this naming power is. We have already begun this in the last chapter, discussing whether life is autonomous from God and nature or is contingent on God. Biomedicine, we saw, essentially ignores the question; it looks only at the mechanisms of life. It is secular bioethics that makes the logical conclusion, declaring each of us to be autonomous, not contingent on God or nature or one another.

3. Illich, *Medical Nemesis*, 20 n.28.

Biomedicine has the power to modify bio-mechanisms; emanating from this the bio-disciplines generally have evolved to take on the role of declaring how important these mechanisms are, and whether there is anything else we need to talk about—in other words, the power of naming what is going on, to the exclusion of all other explanations.

There are many more mundane examples. When a new disease-modifying technology becomes available, we say that people with that disease "need" the technology: diabetics need insulin, people with liver failure need a liver transplant. Biomedicine has the power in Babylon to name what we need. At first this does not look like the "power to name what is going on," but simple facts: diabetics without insulin die; people with untreated liver failure die. The unique naming power of biomedicine is not in these facts, but in transforming them into needs. The person with liver failure will certainly die: is the "need" for a transplanted liver, or for hospice? How openly do those who name what is going on declare that those with transplants are chained for the rest of their lives to the medical system, very likely dying prematurely?

The same is true, more subtly, with diabetes. Today diabetics can live relatively normal lives with insulin; biomedicine's claim that they need insulin does not seem to be a self-serving overstatement, but (again) a simple fact. And it is—for those with the resources to continue buying insulin and monitoring their blood sugars, for those and willing and able to develop the habits of daily drug-taking and monitoring. Not everyone has the resources or can develop these habits. Fully naming what is going on means looking beyond just the mechanisms of disease toward all that is involved in carrying out biomedical treatments. Yet biomedicine, as we have already seen, has chosen to limit its scope to the mechanics of disease only.

When a power such as biomedicine names what is going on, that power often assumes the right to provide the "answer," to be the savior. It is then only a short step to controlling people. It is not necessary to find malicious or manipulative motives in order to call it control: people with liver transplants, who otherwise would be dead, need to be controlled by the medical system in order to stay alive. Most diabetics self-inject their own insulin—but they still remain under the control of their medical care provider, and even more surely under the control of those who manufacture insulin.

## The Wink of Jesus

People who live in any Babylon, including those of us who claim allegiance to the kingdom of heaven, have accepted the power of biomedicine not only to heal but to name what is going on. Biomedicine is for us a principality; we baptize it, we say that God is healing today *through* the power of biomedicine, an interesting syncretism. We have not consciously recognized the difference between the power to modify bio-mechanisms and the power to name what is going on; we open the door to the first, and the second slips in unnoticed. We need to look with fresh eyes at the last healing miracle of Jesus.

Before arriving in Jerusalem for the last time, on his way through Jericho, Jesus encounters two blind beggars and heals them (Matt 20:29–34). This is Matthew's last recorded healing miracle; just after this is the Palm Sunday entrance. John suggests that the raising of Lazarus (in Bethany, closer to Jerusalem than Jericho) comes after the healing of the blind beggar (John 9). After Jesus enters Jerusalem on the donkey, however, his healing work seems to be finished: there are no recorded healing miracles that fit in the usual pattern. All the Gospels record lengthy discourses and parables, but not a lot of action—except that the Synoptic Gospels include Jesus' throwing the money changers, merchants, or both, out of the temple (Matt 21:12; Mark 11:15; Luke 19:45)—and no miracles. Then there is the Last Supper (Matt 26:20–35; Mark 14:17–31; Luke 22:14–38), beginning the final cascade of events culminating in the crucifixion and resurrection.

Now look closely at Jesus' arrest (Matt 26:47–56; Mark 14:43–50; Luke 22:47–54; John 18:3–12). Judas's kiss betrays Jesus to the priests and armed temple guards, who then strong-arm and arrest him. Things must have happened fast right then: before any of the armed guards could stop him, Peter unsheathed his sword and slashed, cutting off the ear of Malchus, a servant of the high priest (see Matt 26:51; Mark 14:47; John 18:10–11)—the right ear, in fact. (Luke 22:50; John 18:10).Was Peter left-handed? Did he strike from behind? Did Malchus bend sharply to the left to avoid the blow? Does it matter?)

Jesus then rapidly defuses the situation: "Put your swords away; all who live by the sword die by the sword. Don't you realize how many angels could rescue me? And don't you yet realize why they aren't here right now? It's all been prophesied: I'm supposed to die." Then he addressed those arresting him: "Why the swords and clubs? Am I a bandit? Why didn't you arrest me while I was teaching during the day?" (Matt 26:47–56, author's paraphrase). Each phrase was a sermon—but at the time the disciples only heard defeat, and ran away, and the guards only heard victory, and led him away.

But right in the middle of this melee, Jesus performs his last healing miracle. He puts back Malchus's ear that had been cut off (Luke 22:51). The disciples may not have been surprised, having seen more magnificent healings, but I wonder what the others thought. They were arresting and getting ready to kill someone who, once again, proved his healing power, his power (ultimately) over death. Did any of them get a little nervous that their plan to limit his power might blow up in their faces? Did they appreciate the irony of threatening with clubs and swords someone who had just miraculously healed one of their own? Did even one of them wonder, "Hey, this might not work"?

With his last healing miracle Jesus, as he is led offstage bound, turns to the audience and winks. What is that wink to us who believe in Jesus, but who have let the impressive achievements of biomedicine substitute for the healing miracles of Jesus today? What is the wink reminding us of when we let biomedicine not only cure us, but also tell us why things happen and name for us what is going on? Where today are the winks of Jesus?

# Chapter 5

# The Beast That Was Healed

## *The Power of Medicine Imitates the Power of God*

SOMETIMES THE BEST WAY to read Revelation is to let a scene affect you visually and emotionally, and not bother initially with what it "means."

Beginning in Rev 12 there is a huge red dragon in heaven, poised to capture and eat the soon-to-be-born son of a pregnant woman. Both the woman and baby escape, and Michael and the other angels attack the dragon, who we are told is the devil, and throw him out of heaven. He is enraged at being defeated, and the earth and sea are warned to beware. For good reason: shortly a beast rises out of the sea, to which the dragon delegates all his power (Rev 13).

Nothing seemed attractive about the dragon, so it is understandable that he would create a proxy. The beast resembles him— both have seven heads and ten horns—but the beast is eventually able to attract a substantial following. It happens this way: somehow he receives a deadly sword wound to one of his heads, recognized by everyone to be fatal. But instead of dying, or perhaps after dying, he recovers; the wound is healed (Rev 13:12). People

43

realize something awesome has happened, and they worship the beast, allowing him free rein. He uses this free rein to boast, utter blasphemies, and make war on the saints (vv. 5–8).

Eventually a second beast emerges, from the earth instead of the sea. This one, later called a false prophet, looks different. He has only two horns like a lamb but sounds like a dragon (Rev 13:11). His primary task seems to be to point to the beast with the fatal wound that had been healed, though he also does his own miracles (vv. 12–13). He even persuades people to set up a statue, an image (*eikōn*) of the beast with the fatal wound that was healed. Then he breathes life into the statue so that it can talk, compelling everyone to worship it—or die (vv. 14–15). Suddenly, the story becomes familiar: everyone was to be branded on the right hand and forehead with the name of this beast with the wound that was healed, or with its number—666. Those without the brand can neither buy nor sell (vv. 16–18).

Those of us claiming allegiance to the kingdom of heaven sometimes find it very tempting to identify the beast, figure out what the number refers to, and nail down when all this will happen. We go right to the *meaning*. But try looking first at the picture. We are in heaven with a hideous dragon (Rev 12:1–4): in the kingdom of heaven there can be no deception—the devil is repulsive. But the same dragon, we are told, deceives the world (12:9). He delegates his authority to a beast who demonstrates power over death (13:1–4), just as Jesus had done with Lazarus (John 11:38–44). The beast may also have been ugly, but having established apparent power over death, this beast can now retire.

A second beast, from the earth, suggestively described in Rev 13 as resembling a lamb but sounding like a dragon (v. 11), now becomes the spokesman (vv. 11–18). He refers back to his predecessor with power over death, and creates once more a distancing from the hideous dragon: a statue of the first beast (likely even more attractive) that he fully controls [vv. 15–16]). Reality becomes virtual reality: more attractive, more controlled, and more controlling. The power over death that gave the beast its fame is not a gift to be shared and multiplied, but a magic trick to be remembered and manipulated.

There is a pattern here we can easily recognize, and perhaps should even look for. In 1 John, we learn that there are antichrists in the plural; not just one Beast or one Antichrist. Are there antichrists in our lives and work? Clearly the fatal wound that is healed in this beast can be a metaphor; but metaphors don't need to be stripped of literal meaning. Might a healed fatal wound resonate with our biomedical responses to fatal diseases?

## Biomedicine as the Beast?

The most obvious and dramatic example in biomedicine of "healing fatal wounds" is CPR, cardiopulmonary resuscitation. In American hospitals, when a patient dies, the default setting of the hospital staff is to perform CPR on the patient—default because CPR will be performed unless there is a specific DNR (Do Not Resuscitate) order in the chart. This is a fascinating end-of-life ritual for biomedicine, uncovering some interesting assumptions. First, death is the ultimate failure for biomedicine, and no one should die unless we in biomedicine have already given up trying, declared the patient unsalvageable, and written a DNR order. But also we continue performing this ritual despite its minimal success: the percentage of patients who survive after CPR is in single digits, or at most in the teens,[1] and the percentage of those who return to healthy living is a tiny fraction of the first figure. CPR is an expensive, pseudoheroic, marginally effective exercise.

But a few patients are "successfully" resuscitated: their vital cardiac and respiratory functions have ceased, and we by our efforts—medicines and maneuvers and machines—restart these vital functions. These people are not on the brink of death; they have died. They have a fatal "wound" which has (temporarily at least) been healed. We are playing God.

Although CPR is the most dramatic of biomedicine's "lifesaving" efforts, it is not the only one, and not the most successful. Much of what we do in intensive care units is to keep death at bay

1. Gallagher et al., "Effectiveness"; Murphy et al., "The Influence."

with our machines and medicines, hoping that our patients will recover. We do the same with mechanical organs (renal dialysis) and vital organ transplants. And far less dramatically, we do the same with replacement medicines such as thyroid hormone and insulin. Without all these efforts, the patients would undoubtedly die. We have (again, temporarily) healed fatal wounds.

Medicine, and even biomedicine, is relatively new at this healing of fatal wounds. All of these developments have come about within the last century—almost all within my lifetime. Throughout history the work of medicine has been the work of healing, using experience, counseling, and plant materials (Sir 38:1–15). Only recently have we been using animal materials (hormones and organ transplants) and machines; only recently have we been trying to reverse death—and only recently have we been succeeding. The logical and expected conclusion is that we are healthier.

However, beginning with René Dubos[2] many writers, Illich among them,[3] have questioned whether or not these sorts of medical advances have made any difference in the overall health of populations, and have concluded they have not. Most infectious diseases, for example, have declined not primarily because of antibiotics or even vaccinations, but because of improvements in nutrition and sanitation. This limited effectiveness of medical intervention is likely even more true with the healing of fatal wounds: a "reversal" of death is certainly dramatic to the individual whose life is "saved," but these reversals, when collected, do not make a difference in the mortality or morbidity of the population as a whole.

Those who understand the mechanisms of disease and biolife may not be surprised to hear this. They know that people need a healthy internal and external environment to thrive; and they know that the mechanics of respiration, for example, can easily be assisted, or even replaced, by machines. Mechanically, the dramatic act of "reversing" death is not nearly as impressive as the achievement of a healthy society. Still, in the popular imagination,

2. Dubos, *Mirage*.
3. Illich, *Medical Nemesis*, chapter 1.

"reversing" death is a miracle, and the ability to do so indicates great power. This may point to the reason that we continue to perform CPR on all dying people despite its minimal success. It is that same popular imagination that gave free rein to the beast whose wound was healed.

## Preventive Medicine and Prevention

The dramatic power of biomedicine to heal fatal wounds has attracted the attention of bioethics, and is likely one reason for the recent marked growth in this discipline. When we in medicine claim to know, and seem to be controlling, the future of a dying person, we all recognize that there are ethical issues at stake. However, biomedicine also claims to know, and tries to control, the future of the entire population of Babylon through preventive medicine, and so far bioethics has had little to say about this. Yet the power implicit in this endeavor rivals the power of the intensive care unit, and eventually will bring us back to the beast in Revelation.

First, however, it is important to clarify the difference between *preventive medicine* and *prevention*, terms which have recently become conflated in Babylon. *Prevention* is the action, attitudes, and style of people and their society that result in those people not getting diseases. *Prevent* as a transitive verb is linked to disease, not health. Admittedly being disease-free can enhance health, but the focus of prevention is disease, both because of the word's meaning and because we closely link health with absence of disease.

Preventing disease in Babylon today is relatively easy to describe but difficult to achieve. It involves (a) what we can accomplish by law (so far mostly sanitation, but also seat belt and antismoking laws), (b) what individual people *choose* to do or not do (mostly having to do with diet and exercise), and (c) what society corporately accepts, promotes, and advertises—the milieu of assumptions about eating, moving, playing, working, loving, and resting, which are not subject to law, but which are often disincentives to healthy living. Clearly *prevention* is not a biomedical matter.

*Preventive medicine*, on the other hand, is. Its goal is not a disease-free society but a disease-free body. Besides providing us with vaccines, it uses its knowledge of biomechanics to find presymptomatic forms of disease (mostly cancer) to treat early before they have done much damage; preventative medicine also seeks to identify biological "risk factors" and to modify them pharmacologically to prevent the development of full-blown disease (especially heart disease). Both involve "screening" the entire population to find out who has these early forms of disease and risk factors.

For example, pap smears and colonoscopies attempt to find early forms of cervical and colon cancer that can be treated surgically before these diseases have spread. Likewise, blood pressure and cholesterol screening identify people with these nonsymptomatic "risk factors" for heart disease, both of which can be modified by taking medicines indefinitely. But note: these are not "replacement" medicines like insulin, and they don't make a person *feel* any better. And although there are general indicators of who to screen (only women of child-bearing age or older get cervical cancer; middle aged and older men are more likely to develop heart disease), these are only the descriptions of who can biologically get the disease. We need to screen everyone in these groups to find who actually has early forms of disease or risk factors.

Yet even after screening everyone, we don't have a clear picture of who will actually get a particular disease. Are all abnormal pap smears and colon polyps precancerous? Will everyone with high blood pressure or high cholesterol get heart disease? The answer is no in each case—but we have at least narrowed down the large groups to those at "high risk," and now our statistics come into play. Because of careful studies on large groups of people, we can determine the probability of which of those with the positive finding will get a particular disease. But only the *probability*: we do not know exactly which person will become ill, only which person will *likely* become ill. If that likelihood is high, we offer treatment for the risk factor.

But what is high likelihood? Ninety-five people out of one hundred getting the condition? Sixty? Forty? How effective is the treatment? Does it *eliminate* the chance of disease, or simply reduce it from, say, 90 percent to 50 percent? Does the treatment have side effects? And most importantly: do I know that I will actually get the disease if I forgo the treatment? Even when all but the last question are clearly answered, I am left only with probabilities. This is strikingly different from saying, "I know I am ill because I have diarrhea or am bleeding or have a painful swelling in my side which the doctor identified as my inflamed liver." Diagnosis based on probabilities is not dia-*gnosis* (literally "through *knowing*") at all. Symptom-based diagnosis has a body: the one who is bleeding. Statistic-based diagnosis is disembodied: there is no specific person who *is* the 25-percent chance.

Let me give some more examples. Two of the most popular screening programs in America today are mammograms for breast cancer in women, and the PSA test for prostate cancer in men. But in Babylon today we do not just treat these as choices or opportunities to remain healthy; they have instead become obligations. Celebrities, especially politicians and government officials, broadcast their health, acting as both examples and warnings. As I write, Elizabeth Edwards, wife of presidential aspirant John Edwards, has just discovered that she has metastatic breast cancer, and has blamed herself because she did not get screening mammograms. But how accurate and effective, how *necessary*, are these screening tests?

Both tests are based on the same assumption: that biomedicine can accurately identify very early forms of cancer, or even precancer—and that treating that cancer saves lives. The mammogram (an X-ray test), and the PSA (a blood test), when abnormal, suggest the need for biopsies—and in both situations, pathologists sometimes identify abnormal cells that may eventually become cancer. But they might not become cancer, and even if they do, the process might take decades—a more important consideration the older the patient is. Still, the conventional wisdom is to remove these cells, and the organ that produced them, *in case* they were cells that would eventually become cancer.

But there is a flaw in this reasoning. Not all cancers are the same: some are very aggressive and are rapidly fatal, while others grow so slowly that we sometimes speak of people dying *with* rather than *from* these cancers—cancers that might be found only incidentally on autopsy, for example. The cancers most likely to be identified in a screening program (mammography or PSA) are slow-growing cancers, sometimes very slow growing.

The most aggressive, fast-growing cancers—the ones that often kill people—might be so fast growing that they could develop and become widespread between annual or biannual screenings test. What this means practically is that not every woman who has a breast removed based on an abnormal mammogram and biopsy would have inevitably developed terminal breast cancer; not every man who undergoes prostatectomy for an abnormal PSA and biopsy was destined to otherwise develop metastatic prostate cancer that would shorten his life.

And now some statistics: Nortin Hadler in *The Last Well Person*[4] reviews several large-scale scientific studies of both mammography and PSA screening, comparing groups of people who were screened with other groups who were not. The benefits of these screening tests are not impressive. Generally, the tests did uncover more people with breast or prostate cancer. But more importantly, the death rates in the two groups in each study were not very different. (And in one large study, there was no increase in detection of breast cancer between the group screened by mammography and the group screened by breast self-exam confirmed by a medical provider.) These screening tests clearly result in more biopsies, more diagnoses of cancer, and more surgical treatments—but not necessarily in longer lives.

But these diagnostic tests and treatments are not harmless. They are very costly; they can be disfiguring (for breast surgery) and have significant side effects of urine leakage and sexual dysfunction—up to 15 percent (for prostate surgery). But equally important, the process—being screened, testing "positive," being treated—labels us all as patients, dependent on biomedicine.

4. Hadler, *Last Well Person*, chapters 4 and 5.

And while this is true of Western biomedicine in all Babylons, it is particularly true in America. Almost none of these studies questioning the value of biomedical screening tests were done in America. Many American professional organizations continue to advocate screening despite evidence from other Western societies (with equal or better health statistics than we have) that much screening is not as beneficial as we would like to believe.

## Statistical Disembodiment

Those who study and make policy for whole populations (and those who gamble) find statistics and probability very useful. But since a statistic has no body, an individual with a body cannot have a statistical dia*gnosis*, but only a probability: a guess, a fear, and an imposed burden. This is the disembodiment we referred to in Chapter 3. When biomedicine makes decisions about screening or treating whole populations because of the statistical risk of disease, it is no longer treating a person with a body.

This statistical disembodiment that routinely separates biomedicine (and its doctors) from individual people with bodies may be new—since the 1980 watershed I described in *Biohealth: Beyond Medicalization; Imposing Health*—but it is only the latest manifestation of biomedicine's progressive disembodiment. Before biomedicine had the power it has now, its practitioners could only talk with patients and touch them. The doctor was not "effective" in manipulating mechanisms but was more effective in establishing a verbal and tactile relationship, a relationship that could sometimes heal. As our dia*gnostic* techniques improved, we could more effectively "know" what was going on inside a person's body, but that required separating a piece of the person's body (a blood sample, a biopsy, an X-ray picture) from the body, a minor form of disembodiment. As we began to gain knowledge of mechanisms, we began to lose the relationship that can heal.[5]

5. Illich, "L'Obsession, 31.

51

Then patients themselves began to understand their own bodies this way, as separate from their essential Self. Seeing a bone spur on an X-ray at the view box separates the pain in my foot from the *meaning* of that pain in the picture. It is a form of disembodying, albeit not complete: my body still has the pain. But having only the *probability* of early heart disease because my cholesterol is a bit high, but I feel fine, is complete disembodiment.

Why is disembodiment a problem? This is an important question, because disembodiment does not diminish biomedical effectiveness. Seeing the X-ray apart from the patient can improve my diagnosis; using statistics judiciously can help me decide what my patient might have based on what other similar patients have had, and select appropriate confirmatory tests. As a biomedical physician, I am not bothered by disembodiment in diagnosis.

But when I, a physician, am also a patient, I begin to understand the problem. When I have a symptom of any sort, I want to know what I *have*, not worry about what statistics tell me I *might* have. And I resist being labeled as a patient (or potential patient) needing to take preventive medicines simply because of my age or gender or other "risk factors"—especially when I present with no "chief complaint." I don't mind being labeled a patient when I feel bad; I do mind being labeled a patient because probability alone tells me I might be on the way to being one.

More than this, disembodied statistics point to the *group* of people at higher risk for the disease, not the specific individuals who will get it. Since we don't know which individuals will get the disease, we treat everyone in the group—meaning we end up treating large numbers of people who do not actually benefit from the treatment (cholesterol-lowering drugs, for example) in order to make sure those who were destined to benefit get the treatment. *Statistically*, the treated group does better, but we cannot know which *individuals* were the beneficiaries. We have even developed a term for this: the NNT—Number Needed to Treat: how many people we need to give the treatment to in order to benefit *one* person. The lower the number, the more obvious the benefit. In preventive medicine, we accept NNTs of fifty to one hundred.

But at heart, disembodiment is a spiritual problem. As we saw in the first chapter, the ultimate leak between the kingdom of heaven and the kingdom of this world is the incarnation: God became embodied, and established a pattern for us. There can be no disembodied spirituality. Everything we do as aliens in the kingdom of this world but as citizens of the kingdom of heaven must be incarnate, must take on flesh. To be disembodied is to be disincarnate. Asking individual people to rely on or submit to disembodied statistics is not consistent with the essence of the incarnation. And to deny the incarnation (1 John 4:2–3) is to be Antichrist. "Well, now he is here, in the world" (v. 3).

The first beast in Rev 13, the one with the fatal wound that is healed, certainly seems to be an antichrist. The second beast, the false prophet, points to the reputation of the first, and his own miracles, to persuade *the people* to set up the statue of the first beast (v. 14). They are not slaves but, as in Aldous Huxley's *Brave New World*, willing participants. The people are impressed by the beasts' apparent miracles and do whatever the beasts tell them (vv. 3, 8, 14–16). Biomedicine has healed fatal wounds, and modern people are impressed: now many willingly go to doctors for preventive medicine. And as they do, biomedicine offers to control their future pharmacologically.

But biomedicine did not begin as a beast (see chapters 2 and 3); it began simply as a method of inquiry. Only within my lifetime has it developed the ability to heal fatal wounds; only within my *professional* lifetime has it offered to control our future. And while doing so bio-ethics arose and pointed to the miracles of biomedicine. But unlike the second beast it did not do miracles of its own or try to persuade people to honor biomedicine. It sat back dispassionately, watched what was gong on, and then summarized what it saw: that there is no contingency on God, that biomedicine and the patients it cares for are autonomous from God.

Now we can come full circle. If we in biomedicine are autonomous from God, we need not worry about disembodied statistics because we have no dealings with an incarnate God. As long as using statistics "works," we use them. We are an evidence-based discipline. As long as fatal wounds are healed, we follow the healer.

We have dealt with the spiritual problem of disembodiment by admitting that biomedicine is not spiritual. And we have finally come to the question posed in the last chapter: whether or not the power to heal automatically confers the power to name what is going on. At first, it would seem to, especially for evidence-based people such as us. Evidence for us confers authority; our biomedical method does not need a proximate or spiritual authority. We follow what works. We apparently no longer believe that we can be deceived; for us there are no dragons and beasts and statues. But maybe we have let them go too quickly.

## Death and Deception

The biblical record ends in Revelation with this story of deception, reminding us to beware. Near the beginning of the biblical record is another story of deception. Moses was sent by God to Pharaoh to demand the release of the Israelites from Egypt (Exod 3—4:17). To demonstrate that Moses was acting according to the power of God, he throws his staff on the ground and it becomes a serpent. But the wizards of Egypt are able to do exactly the same (7:7–13). Likewise with the first two plagues: Moses by the power of God turns the river and canal water of Egypt into blood; then the wizards of Egypt did the same (vv. 20–22). Moses on God's instruction causes frogs to swarm all over the land, and the wizards do the same (8:6–7). These wizards demonstrate extraordinary power; at this point they would seem to have earned the right to name what was going on. Pharaoh agrees.

That, of course, is not the end of the story in Exodus, nor is the branding with 666 the end of the beast story in Revelation. We have not come to the end of the biomedical story either. Moses's serpent eats up the wizards' serpents (Exod 7:12), and he goes on to engineer eight more plagues that the wizards fail to replicate (see Exod 8–12). In Revelation, after a few major battles (see Rev 17–19), the two beasts and eventually the red dragon end up in a lake of burning sulfur (Rev 19:20). The Egyptian wizards and the beasts in the book of Revelation lose their power, and their power to name what is going on. In retrospect, none of them ever has *that* power; what they did have was similar to the power of biomedicine: the power to manipulate mechanisms.

How will the story of biomedicine end? We don't know, and can make no predictions from the other stories because they don't correlate fully with what is going on today. There are flashes of recognition and striking parallels—then the stories and our life part ways. But we are left, like the men on the road to Emmaus, feeling that we just saw something important (see Luke 24:13–35). There is one more story, again from Egypt, which may provide another flash of recognition.

Near the end of his life, Jacob finds himself in a famine. There is food in Egypt, however, so he goes there with his eleven sons and their families; the twelfth, Joseph, is already there, and the extended family all settles in Egypt (see Gen 46). Shortly before dying, Jacob instructs his sons to return his body to the same place where his parents, Isaac and Rebekah, and his grandparents, Abraham and Sarah, are buried. Then Jacob dies (47:29–31; 49:29–33).

Joseph had risen to a fairly high position within Egyptian society, and has access to Egyptian wisdom—remarkable wisdom which had already built the pyramids as much as a thousand years earlier, and had known how to embalm for nearly two thousand years. Even by today's standards, that wisdom was remarkable, and Joseph sees no reason to neglect it. He calls the physicians of Egypt ("physician" is the right English translation, from the Hebrew word "to heal") and provides for his father standard-of-care end-of-life procedures: Joseph has his father embalmed (Gen 50:2–3).

This is a powerful detail. Earlier in Genesis (3:19) we find God's description of bio-death in his statement to Adam after the fall: "for dust you are / and to dust you shall return." The writer of Ecclesiastes (3:20) affirms the same. The tone in the Ecclesiastes comment bespeaks vanity and meaninglessness in life, but the Genesis story provides a deeper context for the sentiment that we return to dust. As we see in Genesis chapter 2, the earth itself brings forth bio-life; God's statement to Adam in chapter 3, verse 19, is straightforward: "you return to the soil as you were taken from it." (The word "return" is key. There is a cycle with bio-life and bio-death, a complete cycle. We return to the earth when we die, but the earth again produces life. We may have played our part, but the cycle goes on; redemption is implied. The very next verse in Genesis chapter 3 after "to dust you shall return" (v. 20) says that Eve is given her name because she is the mother of all who live, or in some translations, "all living."

The writer of Ecclesiastes sees despair in this situation, feelings Joseph may have shared, but Joseph found a way out. By state-of-the-art technology, his father Jacob did not need to return to dust. His body could remain as it was—and today in Abraham's tomb underneath that large tan rectangular mosque/synagogue behind the police station in Hebron in the West Bank, Jacob's mummy may still be entombed together with the bones of his wife Leah, his parents, and his grandparents. Joseph, by technology, had defeated the cycle of life and death. Jacob—also called Israel—remains the same as when he died.

That, of course, was the Israel Jesus confronted: an Israel that had died, with all the life-giving laws shrunken and mummified. We will return to this Israel in chapter 7.

*Part Three*

# Clinical: Healing of Life

" . . . Haven't you heard it said that we ought
to bear one another's burdens?"

"But that means—" she began, and stopped.

"I know," Stanhope said. "It means listening sympathetically, and
thinking unselfishly, and being anxious about, and so on. Well, I
don't say a word against all that; no doubt it helps. But I think when
Christ or St. Paul, or whoever said *bear*, or whatever he Aramaically
said instead of *bear*, he meant something much more like carrying
a parcel instead of someone else. To bear a burden is precisely to
carry it instead of. If you're still carrying yours, I'm not carrying it for
you—however sympathetic I may be. And anyhow there's no need to
introduce Christ, unless you wish. It's a fact of experience. If you give
a weight to me, you can't be carrying it yourself; all I'm asking you to
do is notice that blazing truth. It doesn't sound very difficult."

—CHARLES WILLIAMS, *DESCENT INTO HELL*, 1937

## Chapter 6

## "Your Sins Are Forgiven" /
## "Your Faith Has Made You Whole"

### *The Roots of Healing*

AT FIRST, THE MESSAGE seemed clear. Jesus' fame has begun to spread, both for what he is saying as well as for his healings, and a crowd has gathered at a building in Capernaum to hear him teach, religious leaders included. Some people brought to him a paralyzed man on a stretcher, but since they couldn't squeeze through the crowd with the stretcher, they went onto the roof, removed some roof tiles, and lowered him down right in front of Jesus. "Seeing their faith" (all three accounts include that note), Jesus immediately declares that the man's sins are forgiven. The message clearly is that sin is the man's first problem, presumably the cause of his paralysis (see Luke 5:17–26; see also Matt 9:2–8; Mark 2:3–12).

But the opposite message is even more clear at another healing: the healing of the blind man from the Gospel of John (9:1–41), which we considered in chapter 3. That's when the disciples are trying to clarify whether it is the sin of the blind man himself or the sin of his parents that is the reason for his blindness, and Jesus declares that it is neither (vv. 1–3).

So sin does *not* cause disease. Yet we still haven't gotten to the bottom of Jesus' thinking. A few chapters before the healing of the blind man in John, we hear the story of Jesus healing a man paralyzed for thirty-eight years (5:2–9). After the healing, Jesus tells him not to sin anymore, or something worse will happen to him (v. 14).

## Sin and Forgiveness

Now the message was not at all clear. What is the connection between sin and disease?

In the Old Testament, things seemed more clear. When the wandering Israelites disobey God, they are visited with plagues (Num 12, 17, 21); when they return to God, the plagues are stopped. It had been spelled out in Exod 15:26: following the commandments would prevent the Israelites from getting the diseases that had afflicted the Egyptians, because healing comes from the God of Israel.

Not surprisingly, the New Testament understanding of sin and disease does not turn the Old Testament concept entirely upside-down; Jesus' aim is to fulfill, not abolish, the law. Two of the healing stories above indicate *some* link between sin and disease, and the passage in James about healing (5:14–16) also demonstrates interweaving between the processes of dealing with sin and dealing with illness. The one who is "ill" (*astheneō*, a word for physical disease or weakness) should call for the elders to pray for him, and the prayer will save or restore him (*sōzō*, a word used for both physical and spiritual healing). Therefore, James says, we should confess our sins and pray for each other (clearly spiritual activities) so that we may be healed (*iaomai*, a word for physical healing, related to *iatros*, the word for "physician").

For those of us schooled in biomedicine, this interweaving of physical and spiritual terms seems promiscuous—and for biomedicine, it is. We who assume responsibility for bio-life prefer to keep our categories separate, for that separation between the physical and spiritual was precisely the way that we uncovered physical mechanisms and discovered how to control them. And having discovered those mechanisms, it has become clear to us that our moral and spiritual life has nothing to do with how diseases come about. They are caused by germs or toxins or genes or trauma. Not sin. We like what Jesus says about the man born blind.

Apparently the scribes and Pharisees also want to keep the physical and spiritual categories separate, as specialists in the spiritual. Some come from as far away as Jerusalem to Capernaum, having heard specifically about Jesus' healings, and are in a crowded building when the man on the stretcher descends through the roof. But Jesus refuses to keep the categories separate. When confronted with a man whose obvious problem was physical, he immediately diagnoses and deals with a spiritual problem—to the great consternation of the Pharisees. Not only has Jesus confused their categories, to them he has also blasphemed.

Now Jesus may have been suggesting that the cause of the man's paralysis is his sin, but we don't know this for sure. What we do know is that Jesus diagnoses and treats both the spiritual and the physical problems that the man has. But he clearly is not *only* diagnosing and treating the man; he is also diagnosing and treating the Pharisees. He knows that forgiving sin will intrude on territory they think they know and control, and so, reading their thoughts, Jesus asks which is easier—to forgive sins or heal paralysis?

Then, he says, in order to prove that he has the authority to forgive sins, he heals the paralysis. We still don't know how the sin and paralysis are linked, but it's almost as if Jesus is intentionally redirecting our attention. Jesus is asking the Pharisees to think about disease and sin in ways new to them, yet he still seems to imply that a strict separation of categories—disease and sin—does not fit with reality.

Here is one final note: Jesus doesn't bring up the notion of sin in order to induce guilt, force his patient to admit his disease is his own fault, or maneuver him to plead for forgiveness. Jesus forgives whatever sin is there *without even being asked*. Whatever connection there may be between sin and disease, it is apparently not crucial for the patient to know at the time of healing. In gospel healing miracles, it is not confession of sin that heals; if anything, it is forgiveness of sins, freely offered, that heals.

## Faith and Healing

Now look at the healing of the woman who had the hemorrhage for twelve years (Matt 9:20–22; Mark 5:25–34; Luke 8:43–48). This small story introduces us to all the most important healing words used in the Gospels, and in so doing expands our understanding of biblical healing. When Luke says that no one had been able to cure or heal the woman (v. 43), he uses the Greek word *therapeuō*, which means not only "to cure" but also "to serve," and is related to the word for "attendant." Today we might use the English word "treat" to connote this serving and attending; treatment hopes for, but does not always produce, a cure. (Luke the physician simply admits this failure; Mark the layman goes into much more detail about how she had suffered under the painful treatments of many doctors, had spent all her money, and was getting not better but worse [v. 26])

When she boldly winds her way through the crowd, sneaks up behind Jesus, and touches his cloak, both Mark and Luke say that she is cured or healed (Mark 5:29; Luke 8:47), and the word they use is *iaomai*, the one we saw in the book of James related to the word *physician*. *Iaomai* is what the *iatros* does, or hopes to do. But in this case the *iatros* did not take a history or perform a physical exam. He was on his way to a house call for a dying twelve-year-old girl but immediately knew when someone accessed his power (Mark 5:30; Luke 8:46). It was then that the woman becomes fearful; she had apparently hoped for an anonymous healing, but Jesus stops and begins searching through the crowd for the one who had been healed (Mark 5:32).

She comes forward trembling, tells Jesus exactly what happened (Mark 5:33; Luke 8:47), and he says, "Your faith has made you whole"—whole or healthy or well (Matt 9:22; Mark 5:34; Luke 8:48). The word is *sōzō*, the one we saw in James that is used for both physical and spiritual healing, and is often translated "saved." (Twice more Jesus uses the same sentence—"Your faith has made you whole"—once for a leper [Luke 17:19] and again for a blind man [Mark 10:52]: in each case the word is *sōzō*. Earlier in Luke as well [7:50] a form of *sōzō* appears when Jesus utters this same sentence to forgive a sinful woman who is anointing his feet and wiping them with her hair; this occurrence of *sōzō* shows, as we will soon see below, that for Jesus and his contemporaries the concept of health entails more than physical restoration.) In Matthew's account of the woman with the hemorrhage, the same word, *sōzō*, is used not only for the outcome of the woman's faith (being made whole) but also for what she was seeking in touching Jesus' cloak, as well as the result of that touching (see Matt 9:22).

Mark's account of this episode then adds one more phrase to Jesus' blessing which gives us a fourth healing word: "Go in peace and be free from your complaint" (5:34). This word for healing is *hugiēs*, and means "sound," "whole," or "healthy." It is usually used for physical health—but again, the categories are blurred. In the Gospel of John Jesus warns the man who has been healed after thirty-eight years of paralysis, he says, "Now that you are healthy (*hugiēs*), be sure that you don't sin anymore, or something worse may befall you" (5:14 RSV). The man is physically healthy but is given a spiritual instruction to remain that way. The man is physically healthy but is given a spiritual instruction to remain that way.

## Holistic Healing

The obvious lesson from all of these healing stories is that biblical healing is holistic. Yet holistic healing is not a new approach for some sectors of biomedicine. Over the last generation we have talked, especially in family medicine, about the bio-psycho-social approach to treatment. More recently it is becoming acceptable to include spirituality in the list of factors that influence health. And to many outside of biomedicine, this blurring of categories that Jesus insisted on with the paralyzed man let down through the roof (Matt 9:2–8; Mark 2:1–12; Luke 5:17–26), is very welcome and long overdue. Intuitively most laypeople know that emotions can cause physical symptoms, for example, and that guilt can make a person ill. The widespread growth of complementary and alternative medicine is further evidence that people are not satisfied with the narrow focus and reductionism of biomedicine.

We in biomedicine listen to this critique—sort of. We are very happy to have family medicine put a human face on biomedicine, to create a user-friendly vehicle for our ultra-high-tech products, to be the lamb-like beast with two horns instead of ten (see Rev 13:1–2, 11). We are glad too for these generalist-specialists who will deal with the softer, messier parts of ill-health that don't lend themselves easily to mechanical manipulation. We know very well that dis-ease is far more than bio-disease, but we didn't go to medical school to heal society, we went to learn techniques of biomedicine. Because ultimately, biomedicine truly does have powers over bio-mechanisms that outstrip those of most forms of complementary and alternative medicine, or contemporary religion. We may sound like a dragon to some who are frustrated by our depersonalized care, but we can heal fatal wounds.

If America—or any Babylon—would like biomedicine to be more holistic, it is time to admit: this is not possible. Biomedicine made a Faustian deal at its origin. It followed the techniques that allowed it to manipulate bio-mechanisms, techniques that give it great power—power even to cure disease. But the trade-off was that it had to ignore the true origins and causes of disease and focus only on the mechanisms—or symptoms. You cannot look through a microscope and a telescope at the same time.

Yet we have convinced ourselves that bacteria or viruses or genes or toxins or trauma *are* the true origins of disease. Of course we know that these germs and insults come from *somewhere*, but knowing where does not help us manipulate bio-mechanisms and treat the symptoms; we will let public health and politics and religion chase down the sources. We have found ways of eliminating the disease without eliminating the source—which really means that we can eliminate only the symptoms of the disease in the person since we haven't gotten to the source. Just as our biomedicine is autonomous from God, it is also autonomous from ultimate causes. Mechanism medicine is only symptom-control medicine because the roots of disease are never in the mechanisms.

## Sin and Sickness

Now we can return to Jesus and the windows into true healing that he provided for us. Jesus told the disciples that it was neither the man's sin nor his parents' that caused his congenital blindness. The disciples were asking the wrong question, he said, and so are we if we are trying to define a cause-and-effect relationship between a person's specific sin and their specific disease. That exercise is not helpful. However, the lack of a one-to-one relationship between sin and sickness does not automatically remove sin from the discussion. With the man paralyzed thirty-eight years, and the man let down through the roof, Jesus strongly implied some connection. Perhaps his comments were drawn from an understanding of sin in general being at the root of all disease, the ultimate cause which biomedicine chooses to ignore. But there is no sin in general; sin is always incarnate, embodied; in the man lowered through the roof Jesus forgives a specific man, and in the man healed after thirty-eight years Jesus warns another specific man not to sin anymore.

There is a further lesson in "Your faith has made you whole." Each time Jesus says this, he has been vigorously pursued by the one healed: the woman with the hemorrhage (Matt 9:20–21; Mark 5:27–28; Luke 8:43–44); the Samaritan leper, one out of ten, who deliberately returns to Jesus to thank him (Luke 17:15–19); and Bartimaeus, the blind man who shouts out to Jesus to have pity on him (Mark 10:46–52). Each time the mechanism of disease is corrected without any particular hygiene or medication or technique involved. And each time Jesus declares the person "saved" or safe or well—a word suggesting more than simply the elimination of the mechanisms of disease, used more often biblically in a spiritual than physical sense. More than this, it is *their* faith—quite unrelated to the mechanisms of disease—that has made them well; they have actively participated in their own healing. For each, correcting the mechanism of disease is only a part of their becoming well.

Navajo Indians know this. I visited a "sing"—a several-day healing event—for a Navajo man that had some stubborn symptoms that doctors had been unable to eliminate. The evening event

I attended was a traditional meal prepared and shared by dozens, possibly a hundred, of his relatives and neighbors, and was followed that night by chants and prayers of the medicine man. To my surprise, the patient himself was the host at the meal, welcoming each guest: he was not a passive patient, but an active participant in his own healing ceremony.

## Biomedicine and Listening

Now let's return for a moment to biomedicine's attempt to practice holistic healing. In developing a bio-psycho-socio-spiritual model, family medicine is attempting to go beyond biomedicine, to admit what Jesus demonstrated, that the roots of disease are more than the germs or toxins or imbalances we manipulate inside a person's body. The problem is that the only power we really have is to manipulate those body mechanisms, because family medicine is part of biomedicine. We can recognize the roots of disease, but we can't change them. Yet many of our patients know this, and surprisingly they are not asking for us to; they simply want us to listen.

A recent story from my experience illustrates: While I was working in a walk-in clinic one day, a patient who usually sees another doctor came for an unscheduled visit. I listened to his problem, and at the end of the visit, he said, "You understand my problem. My doctor doesn't. I want to change and have you be my doctor." The irony is that I didn't really understand his problem; and the doctor he was referring to, besides being very nice, was much more current than I, recently out of his family medicine training. But it is precisely for that reason—that he was more current than I—that he had less time to listen to his patient. He had to do all that the standard of care requires he do, including preventive activities. Unfortunately, he had no time left to listen.

Listening is an important *therapeuō*, an excellent way to serve or attend to our patients—and sometimes results in "cure" or "healing," which are the common translations for this Greek word. But listening manipulates no bio-mechanisms, and more significantly in our market-driven biomedicine, sells no drugs. And as important as listening is, it does not by itself deal with the roots of disease—though it can allow the patient to discover them. Listening is what we can offer, and it can be very helpful to patients, but it is a small part of holistic healing. When listening heals, it heals in spite of biomedicine, not because of it.

But there is a more sinister side to the manipulations of biomedicine, manipulations that ignore root causes. We suggested in Chapter 3 that disease is but a symptom of something disordered in the cosmos, something we are calling here sin. Biomedicine is able to manipulate only the individual with the symptoms of this disorder, not the disordered cosmos itself. Therefore we risk causing an imbalance by changing one part without changing the whole.[1] Or said differently: biomedicine surgically or chemically enables a person to live with less distress in a diseased world, without changing that world. More bluntly, we change sick *people* so they can live in the sick world we can't change.[2] We give an office worker pain medicine for an occupationally acquired tendonitis instead of changing her daily repetitive tasks; we dispense condoms and birth control to a teenager with self-destructive sexual habits without even mentioning the possibility of faithfulness to one partner or abstinence; we treat diabetes with medicine when weight loss "fails."

In Chapter 2 we proposed that bio-life is but a tangible image, an *eikōn*, of spiritual Life, but when bio-life becomes for us all of Life, it becomes an idol—*eidōlon*. For biomedicine, bio-life *is* all of Life; the best biomedicine can do is try to adjust that bio-life to the disordered world that has caused the disease in the first place. Biblical healing, on the other hand, still recognizes that bio-life is but a part of Life. When the body was diseased, Jesus sought to make a connection between the diseased person and the source of Life; he engineered leaks between the kingdom of heaven and the kingdom of this world.

But these leaks had been going on long before Jesus. Look at the very first healing miracle in the Gospels. Elizabeth and

1. Ellul, *Presence*, 133.
2. Illich, *Medical Nemesis*, 169; Illich, *Brave New Biocracy*.

Zechariah are a devout Israelite couple, she a descendant of Aaron, he a priest. Unfortunately they are infertile and have gotten to an age when no one thought they would be able to conceive. Infertility today is a major disappointment; then it was even worse—a disgrace: and consequently Elizabeth and Zechariah had prayed desperately for a child. Their prayer is eventually answered miraculously: Elizabeth, in her "old age" (Luke 1:36) became pregnant and delivers a son, John the Baptist (see Luke 1:5–25, 57–66).

This first healing miracle of the New Testament has a pattern worth considering. Elizabeth doesn't simply find herself pregnant, nor does she take an herb or consult with a prophet. That would have simply dealt with the mechanics of the problem. God instead is concerned that she and Zechariah have a window to the larger picture, that they experience a leak between the kingdom of heaven and the kingdom of this world. The angel Gabriel himself comes to Zechariah while he is serving in the temple, and announces to him that he will have a son. But not just any son: this son will come with "the spirit and power of Elijah" and will prepare people for the coming of the Messiah (Luke 1:10–17). The healing of their infertility is a part of something much larger.

We find elements of the same pattern, though more subtly, later on in Luke (7:11–16) with one of the healings of Jesus. Still relatively early in his public life, in the town of Nain in Galilee, Jesus encounters a funeral procession for a young man, the only son of a woman who is a widow. As in many traditional cultures, this woman will now be doubly blighted: childless and with no husband—with no family at all. Jesus raises her son from the dead. That is the mechanical part.

But Luke gives us some clues that this healing is part of something larger. He tells us that after the raised man began to talk, Jesus "gave him to his mother" (v. 15 RSV) Here Luke is quoting from the story of Elijah's first healing miracle, a healing nearly identical to the one Jesus had just performed (see 1 Kgs 17:17–24). Once again, there is a connection with this odd prophet, who, together with Moses, joined Jesus at the transfiguration (another wonderful leak [Matt 17:1–13; Mark 9:2–10; Luke 9:28–36]). And more than

68

this, Luke tells us that the people witnessing this miracle recognize that a great prophet is among them—in fact, they say, "God has visited his people" (7:16 NASB). This is a revealing of Emmanuel, God with us. This is, as we said in Chapter 1, the ultimate leak between the kingdom of heaven and the kingdom of this world. This is the incarnation.

## Chapter 7

# Healing on the Sabbath

## *The Essence of Healing*

SABBATHS MAKE UP 14 percent of days, one out of seven; of the recorded healing miracles of Jesus, about 28 percent occur on the Sabbath, nearly one in three. Jesus seems to preferentially heal on the Sabbath, the one day the religious leaders prohibit all work, including healing. Virtually all the Gospel references to the Sabbath, except those referring to Jesus' burial, are concerned with healing miracles. Looking at this connection between Jesus' healings and the Sabbath may help bring us a step closer to understanding the nature of biblical healing.

The first few recorded healing miracles, the casting out of the demon that we saw in Chapter 3 (Mark 1:21–28; Luke 4:31–37) and the healing of Peter's mother-in-law from fever immediately following (Mark 1:29–31; Luke 4:38–39), are Sabbath healings, with apparently no ensuing debate with the Pharisees. These miracles are in Galilee, early in Jesus' public life; possibly the Jerusalem religious leadership hadn't heard much about him yet. But it didn't take long for the Sabbath debate to get heated. Mark and Luke place the first major debate even before the official choosing of the twelve apostles (Mark 3:17; Luke 6:14).

We saw in Chapter 6 that the Pharisees had already taken issue with Jesus during the healing of the paralytic man let down through the roof. (Matt 9:2–8; Mark 2:1–12; Luke 5:17–26). After that, they are needling him about associating with sinners, and his response must have given them pause. It isn't the healthy, he says, who need a doctor, but the sick (Matt 9:12–13; Mark 2:17–18; Luke 5:31–32) (In those days this was still true; preventive medicine hadn't been invented yet.) Jesus didn't come to call the virtuous, but sinners. At first, the Pharisees may have thought this was a compliment, for they knew they were virtuous.

A short time later, on a Sabbath, Jesus and his disciples are walking through a grainfield, and his disciples are gleaning grain. Gleaning was permitted in the law, but the Pharisees have some difficulty with them gleaning on the Sabbath. This is when Jesus engages the Pharisees in some fine points of interpretation in the law, and then declares himself master even of the Sabbath (Matt; 12:1–8; Mark 5:23–28; Luke 6:1–5). But Mark adds to this one small sentence that is not in Matthew or Luke: "The Sabbath was made for man, not man for the Sabbath"(5:27)—a sentence we'll return to shortly.

Finally we get to the healing itself, not one of Jesus's most spectacular. It is again on a Sabbath day in the synagogue, and the Pharisees are watching closely to see if Jesus will cure the man there with a nonfunctional, dried up right hand (Matt 12:9–14; Mark 3:1–6; Luke 6:6–11). More than just watching, Matthew says that they ask Jesus whether or not it is against the law to heal on the Sabbath (12:10). Jesus knows exactly what is happening, and walks right into it. He tells the man to come into the very middle of the people (Mark 3:3; Luke 6:8), and then asks them all: "Is it against the law on the Sabbath to do good, or to do evil; to save life, or to destroy it?" It is a straightforward question, but the Pharisees must have seen the trap, for no one answers him. Then he tells the man simply to stretch out his hand, and when he does, the hand is restored—and the Pharisees' plot to destroy Jesus is hatched.

Hidden within this story are a fascinating wordplay and a rich irony. All three Gospel writers use the same word for what the Pharisees are watching for: whether or not Jesus will cure (*therapeuō*) the man on the Sabbath, and whether or not this is legal (Matt 12:10; Mark 3:2; Luke 6:7).*Therapeuō*, we have seen, means not only cure, but also serve; it is what an attendant does. Clearly this kind of curing connotes work, and the Pharisees (the "Sabbath police" of the day) were out to enforce 'no work' on the Sabbath. But Jesus, in his response, uses one of the other healing words: he asks whether it is against the law to save life, or destroy it—and for "save life" he uses the word *sōzō*, which we have seen can refer to both physical and spiritual healing. Once again, Jesus purposely muddles the boundary between the two. He shifts the focus from the work of curing to the result of saving life.

The irony appears when we conflate the accounts of Mark and Luke, which I have done above. In Luke's account Jesus asks, "Is it against the law on the Sabbath to save life, or destroy it?" (6:9). After Jesus decides to save life, Mark tells us that the Pharisees begin discussing how to destroy Jesus, hatching their plot on the Sabbath itself for destroying life (3:6). It's the same word for *destroy* that appears in Luke in Jesus' question to the Pharisees.

## The Sabbath as Creation

But why is the Sabbath so important, both to the Pharisees in trying to ensure that no work is done, and in Jesus' preferentially choosing the Sabbath to heal? There may be many reasons, but a simple reading of the Ten Commandments is revealing. The fourth commandment ("Remember the Sabbath day . . .") is the longest, both in Exodus (20:8–11) and in Deuteronomy (5:12–15). A few other commandments—the one about idol-making especially but also those on honoring parents and coveting—have some other explanatory material, but not to the extent that the Sabbath commandment does. Half of the explanation details exactly who should keep the Sabbath: essentially everyone, including animals. It's in the other half where we find some clues about the uniqueness of this commandment.

In Exodus, the Sabbath command refers back to creation (20:11). All the other commandments have as their context the situation of people *after* the fall: the tendency to follow other gods, to make images of them, and to treat one another horribly. The Sabbath commandment is rooted in God's creative activity *before* the fall, which we are told repeatedly in Gen 1 was good, and in the respite and rest that followed creation. The other commandments seem intended to constrain our fallen tendencies; the Sabbath commandment seems the opposite, intending to expand our memory of what was originally good.

In Deuteronomy (5:15), however, there is a different explanation of what the Sabbath is for—the only place where the commandments differ in the two accounts. Here we find the command linked to the Israelites' liberation from Egypt. But this doesn't contradict Exodus, it enriches it: God is both creator and redeemer. Because we are fallen, we need to constrain our behavior; but constraining alone does not make us good. We need to remember and follow the pattern God established for creating *and* redeeming, and apparently the best way to remember is to rest.

Now we can come back to the small comment that Mark inserts into the discussion of gleaning on the Sabbath: "The Sabbath was made for man, not man for the Sabbath" (5:27). The Sabbath, Jesus is saying, is a gift. The Pharisees have taken this gift and dried it up, making it into a useless obligation—much like the man's dried up right hand that Jesus restores. The Pharisees had made the law, not people, the focus, and tried to squeeze people into their interpretation of the law.

Jesus sees that they have turned the law upside-down, and he is trying to right it. People are the focus, he says; the Sabbath, and by implication all of the law, is a gift for people's benefit. The point of Sabbath-keeping is not to satisfy an abstract law, let alone God ("If I were hungry, I would not tell you / . . . / Do I eat the flesh of bulls"? [Ps 50:12]). The law, symbolized by the Sabbath, was made for us, so that we can become and remain whole and healthy.

This lesson is clear in the healing of the man at the pool of Bethzatha, to which we have referred several times (John 5:1–18).

The man has been paralyzed for thirty-eight years, yet he is staying at the healing pool with all sorts of other blind, lame, and paralyzed people. It must have been like a modern nursing home: a biomedical facility for all the people biomedicine has failed to help. And as in the nursing home, some people at the pool still voiced a sort of pathetic hope that maybe they would be able to get into the pool first the next time the angel comes, and be healed. Our man seems to have given up—he is paralyzed, and so cannot move quickly to the pool when the angel comes. Yet Jesus found him, hopeless, at the place of healing.

Once again, like so many others, this healing miracle has nothing to do with technique. Jesus simply tells the man to stand up and walk, which he does. The significance here is not in how Jesus heals but in the healing words that John uses. Throughout the story, John uses the word *hugiēs*, which we saw means "to be sound, whole, or healthy." Over half of the uses of this word in the New Testament refer to this one story. However, when the "Sabbath police" come to investigate (this healing takes place on the Sabbath), John says they interview the man who has been cured (*therapeuō*). They keep harping on the technique, which they see as involving work; John makes it clear that the miracle is about health and wholeness. Two chapters later, Jesus spells it out to his critics: "Why are you angry at me for making a man whole (*hugiēs*) on the Sabbath?" (7:23).

## The Source of Life

It is clearly appropriate to heal on the Sabbath, but what does this have to do with biomedicine? To enter this question, let us briefly recapitulate the central argument of the book so far. We saw that the power of biomedicine is not contingent on God: autonomous, and its power is contingent only on the ability to manipulate biological mechanisms. Biomedicine uses its significant power to eliminate symptoms of disease, prolong biological life, and name what is going on in human bodies. Part of this naming is the presumption of knowing the future by statistical analysis, and then controlling the future through preventive medicine.

However, since this power of biomedicine is only an imitation of true healing power, it is limited. It has no link with spiritual realities. It can never be truly holistic because it cannot address the real causes of disease or give disease meaning (see chapter 9 on metaphor, below). Instead it offers disembodied solutions and intervenes in a disease process only partially, but enough to cause historical, cultural, and spiritual ways of healing to atrophy. Biomedicine does to healing what the Pharisees did to Sabbath-keeping, shrinking it from a rich gift to a technique they could control.

The point of the Sabbath is certainly to rest: to renew, restore, and recreate. The land itself is also to lie fallow and have a "Sabbath rest" every seventh year, and the entire people is to have a year of renewal every fiftieth year—the Jubilee Year (Lev 25). According to the Torah, rest is important for the health of the land and the people as well as for each individual. But Sabbaths are also meant to remind the people of their Creator and Redeemer; likely one of the reasons for resting was to free the mind to remember.

The problem with autonomous biomedicine is that it has no Sabbath because it has no reference point in creation and redemption. Sabbath-keeping was never meant to be a rule-laden obligation; instead it offers a connection to the source of Life. But for biomedicine there is no Life, only bio-life; there is no memory, only technique; there is no rest, only research.

Look at biomedicine's chronic disease model of health care. This model says that chronic diseases can be controlled by taking mediations daily. Not long ago I read that less than half of Americans with high blood pressure have it adequately controlled. More recently, in a medical review of diabetes, I encountered the remarkable statement that nationally, only "few" patients with diabetes have controlled their sugars adequately. Why?

One of my professors in my family medicine training had had diabetes since he was thirteen years old. By the time he was teaching me, he had begun to develop changes in his eyes due to the diabetes and so needed laser treatments. He invited me to accompany him to see what was involved. That was thirty years ago. He had controlled his sugar so well throughout his life that by his late seventies, when he died, it was not from the common complications: kidney failure, a heart attack, or amputations. It was, rather, from a lung cancer unrelated to diabetes. He lived so long precisely because of the power of biomedicine, and because he had adhered well throughout his life with the medical treatments for his chronic disease.

He is, unfortunately, unusual. A commonly quoted figure is that roughly only half of patients adhere faithfully to any medical treatments. Some years ago I worked on the Navajo Indian reservation, where diabetes is very common, possibly affecting a third of the people there. Yet, despite free medical care and free medications, approximately half of the people we cared for had poor control of their diabetes.

What causes this large but partial "failure"—a story that could be repeated in so many places for so many other chronic diseases, from asthma and AIDS to high blood pressure and heart failure? There are several possible causes:

1) **The medicines themselves.** While it is certainly true that they don't eliminate the problem, they have "proven" effectiveness in controlling many diseases (as in the case of my family medicine professor). Yet their "success" in practice does not mirror this proven effectiveness.

2) **Cost.** Cost—for medications, the office visit, and transport—is clearly one reason some people fail to control their chronic diseases. But it is unlikely the primary reason: the failure rate for diabetes control among Navajos is similar to the failure rate in other American populations, yet with Navajos cost is not a factor.

3) **The treatment plan.** What we ask patients to do to control their disease—to make activity modifications and dietary changes, to take medications according to schedule, and to make frequent clinic visits—varies greatly according to the disease, ranging from only one pill a day and a yearly doctor

visit to very complex regimens. And patients themselves vary, from being very disciplined (my family medicine professor) to being completely noncooperative. We need to look more closely at the nature of biomedicine's treatment plans.

Successful chronic disease care depends on an active, involved, and often literate patient. This is exactly the opposite of successful surgery, which depends on a passive patient—in fact an unconscious patient. Yet in both cases, biomedical "miracles" work best when we biomedical practitioners control everything, or (for chronic disease care) when our patients internalize that control. Conversely, biomedical treatments of any type fare poorly when they are done incompletely: when surgeons ignore sterile technique, or when diabetics try to control their disease without changing their diet or activity. Said perhaps too simply, biomedical treatments only work when they are done right.

In most Babylons, biomedicine maintains control over its practitioners through licensing, but it has no comparable control over its patients. We therefore rely on "patient education": encouragement and persuasion. These techniques ought to work, and sometimes they do. But still, up to half of patients with chronic diseases do not have their diseases under control. Why?

The half figure that keeps cropping up is mirrored by another haunting American statistic: as many as half of Americans have basic or below-basic literary skills—meaning their literacy is less than what is necessary to identify the main purpose of a newspaper article, to identify a location on a map, or to calculate the total cost of office supplies ordered from a catalog. And, to make explicit the connection to health, that half is generally less healthy: several research studies have shown low literacy to be associated with less healthy behaviors and poorer health.[1] Clearly lower literacy may be linked with lower socioeconomic status, a factor that Nortin Hadler says is responsible for 75 percent of ill health and premature death in America.[2]

1. Wallace et al., "Brief Report."
2. Hadler, *Last Well Person*, 11–12.

This is not to say that poverty is the only reason for the lack of patient success in chronic disease care: it isn't. What biomedicine asks of all patients in controlling their own chronic diseases is a huge undertaking, one that requires sometimes immense focus and commitment—and understanding. Not all highly literate patients are willing or able to make that kind of commitment, even though failing to do so will likely shorten their lives. It is really no surprise that Americans with less educational and financial resources, and sometimes with more urgent family, legal, or emotional priorities, may "fail" to make full use of biomedicine's offerings in controlling their diseases.

But there are of course those patients—maybe half of them—who succeed in controlling their diseases. They exonerate the chronic disease model; the problem must be within the individual patients who fail. We in biomedicine have become like Pharisees, demonstrating with our model patients that it *is* possible to follow the law of adherence to medical regimes, and requiring (only we call it "encouraging") our noncompliant patients to do the same.

We provide abundant "patient education" for personal control of disease, much as the Pharisees had voluminous requirements for Sabbath-keeping. But Jesus, the one who showed such little regard for their Sabbath regulations, whose power of healing exceeded theirs, called the regulations they loaded on people "burdens that are unendurable" (Luke 11:46). Apparently the same is true for our treatments for many patients with chronic diseases in America and other Babylons. Biomedicine, like the Pharisees, has no real Sabbath connecting it with connected to the source of Life, only Sabbath regulations.

We need another way to see chronic disease. Look at these Sabbath healing miracles Jesus performed on his last journey into Jerusalem, which in Luke begins halfway through his Gospel. In chapters 13 and 14 we find the healing of two people with chronic diseases. The first is a woman with a back problem, "bent double" and unable to stand upright for eighteen years (13:10–17). She has come to synagogue to worship, and when Jesus sees her, he calls her over, lays his hands on her, and tells her to stand up straight, which she promptly does.

As usual, this causes a stir among the religious leaders, and this time the synagogue official addresses his comments to the people present, telling them not to come for healing on the Sabbath—there are six other days in the week for that, he tells them. Jesus points out the inconsistency of this argument—they of course "work" to untie their animals for watering on the Sabbath—but then got right to the point. This woman had been bound by her infirmity, by Satan in fact, for eighteen years: what better time to loose these bonds than on the Sabbath, the day of remembering the Creator and Redeemer?

Jesus connects this woman to Life itself; there is no requirement for daily medications, no special diets, no burdensome exercise routine. Luke underlines this freedom with parables on either side of the healing. Just before the healing, Jesus tells a story about a fig tree that produces no fruit for three years. It is unsuccessful, sterile, and useless, but it is still alive. (13:6–9).

The tree is, like the woman, bound. The man who planted the tree suggests it be cut down, but the gardener disagrees; he wants one more season to care for it and fertilize it. The gardener is like today's caretakers in the chronic disease model of biomedicine: when confronted with our failures, we resist facing the obvious— that the model just isn't working, and that the glorious successes are the exceptions that prove the rule. Let us keep trying, we say.

Then right after the healing, Jesus asks, "But what is the kingdom of God like?" and makes a striking comparison to the sterile fig tree. Jesus says the kingdom is like a mustard seed "thrown" into a garden, which grows into a magnificent tree, big enough for birds to perch in the branches (13:18–19). Or, he says, like yeast put into dough, which makes the whole loaf rise (13:20–21). There is no gardener here, fine-tuning his techniques, advocating for "one more chance"; instead there is life, real Life, unbound, unattended, free.

There is a similar lesson in the very next healing in Luke's Gospel. Jesus is at the house of a Pharisee for a meal on a Sabbath, and a man is present who has "dropsy," edema or swelling in his legs and possibly in his abdomen as well (14:1–6). There are several possible reasons for this kind of swelling: heart failure, kidney disease, or a badly scarred liver—all of them chronic, incurable conditions. I suppose it could have been elephantiasis from lymphatic blockage, also chronic and incurable.

This time the Pharisees are watching Jesus closely, so he brings up the topic: "Is it lawful to heal on the Sabbath?" (14:3 RSV)—and this time he tackles the "work" of treatment directly, because the word he uses is *therapeuō*, the word that is related to serving. The Pharisees have no answer, so he physically heals (*iaomai*) the man. Then, after pointing out the Pharisees' hypocrisy—that they would of course pull their son out of a well he had fallen into on the Sabbath—Jesus seems to change the subject.

## Who Is Honored?

Jesus notices how the invited guests have chosen to sit at the places of honor, and gives them some practical advice: it's better to choose the lower places initially, because if you get it wrong and choose a place too high, you'll embarrass yourself (14:7–10). But of course his fundamental interest is not banquet etiquette; it is about exalting oneself: "Everyone who exalts himself will be humbled, and the man who humbles himself will be exalted" (v. 11). His comments may have been aimed at those who had assumed "higher places" of understanding regarding the Sabbath, who thought they knew what it meant.

But could the comments also be aimed at those of us in biomedicine who "know" the best way to handle chronic disease?

## Chapter 8

# "He Carried Our Diseases"

## *The Way of Healing*

ALL OF THE GOSPEL writers tell us that Jesus healed far more people than the two dozen or so we have details about. Matthew tells us this at least five times, and the second time is right after Jesus cures the fever of Peter's mother-in-law: "That evening they brought him many who were possessed by devils. He cast out the spirits with a word and cured all who were sick" (8:16–17). Mark and Luke also tell us this, but only Matthew adds that these healings are to fulfill a prophesy of Isaiah (8:17).

The quote is from Isa 53, the section commonly referred to as the Suffering Servant, and the specific verse is the one which says, "He has borne our griefs [or sufferings] and carried our sorrows" (v. 4 RSV). But Matthew translates this "He himself took our infirmities [or sicknesses] and carried our diseases" (8:17 RSV). Has Matthew inappropriately medicalized the Suffering Servant?

No. The Hebrew word translated as "griefs" or "sufferings" actually means "sickness"; the word translated as "sorrows" actually means "pain." Matthew's, and the resulting English translations of the Greek, seem closer to the Hebrew than the usual Old

Testament renderings. Isaiah himself may have wanted us to reflect on generic sufferings and sorrows, but it appears that he also had diseases in mind. Isa 53:3 could read, "He was a man of pain, and acquainted with sickness"; verse 5 says that as a result of the scourgings of the Suffering Servant, we are "healed"—a word used for physical healing in the history books of the Old Testament.

However, the accuracy of the medicalized translation in Matthew presents us with a problem: how does one person carry someone else's disease? If what is meant are general sufferings and sorrows, we can imagine empathizing with another and entering into their sorrow. *Compassion*, in fact, literally means "with suffering" or "to suffer with." But carrying someone's *disease* doesn't make sense.

Some of the modern translators must have also felt uncomfortable with this, and solved the problem by telling us in Matthew that Jesus "took our sicknesses *away*" (JB) and "carried *away* our diseases" (NASB). But these renderings sanitize a troubling text: the words for "take" and "carry" in both Hebrew and Greek mean just that: the first is "to lift, take or receive"; the second, "to take up or bear a heavy load, to carry."

Further, when we consider Isa 53, the Servant does not "carry away" our infirmities; he bears them along with our sins and iniquities (vv. 11,12) and is crushed by them (vv. 5,10). This is not transporting away something unpleasant, like carrying out the garbage; this is not eliminating by a magic wand or by fiat. Our sins cannot be so easily dispensed with, nor can our diseases.

We have come to the heart of the matter, to a climax in the conversation between biomedicine and biblical healing. The claim of biomedicine is that adjusting the mechanisms of disease manages or cures the disease; the suggestion of Matthew is that disease is like sin, and it is cured only by someone carrying it for us.

Assume for a moment that Matthew is right. In his day, Jesus carried the sicknesses and diseases of people, and they were made whole. In our day, with the ascendancy of biomedicine, no one tries to carry disease in the same way. In the last two chapters we have suggested that biomedicine's contributions, while powerful, are not complete; that biomedicine effectively removes symptoms of disease, but by its very nature cannot get to the roots. Do we need to settle for this "lower standard of care" than the one Jesus practiced?

## Biblical Carrying Stories

There is a "back door" way to get at this question, and that is by looking at the wisdom of non-Western cultures, as we did in Chapter 3. Some traditional cultures have selected people with certain diseases to be the healers; in others, those in the process of becoming healers experience many symptoms of illness.[1] In some ways, these healers have already "carried" the diseases they were being prepared to treat. Likewise, some traditional cultures allow infertile women to accompany midwives as they work, even apprenticing them.

Though it is only conjecture, this may have been the case for the Israelites enslaved in Egypt. The Egyptian king orders the midwives to kill all baby boys in an attempt to reduce the threat of the future Israelite nation to the Egyptians (Exod 1:15–16). The Israelite midwives disobey the king (vv. 17–19) and are rewarded by God, who "gave them families of their own" (vv. 20–21 NIV). This suggests that they do not already have families. Possibly infertile midwives would be the most able to "suffer with" a woman who delivers a stillbirth or who loses a child shortly after birth.

There is just a hint of this carrying, or at least identifying with the one being healed, in the healing stories of Elijah and Elisha. Early in his prophetic life, Elijah is staying with a widow and her only son. When the boy dies, Elijah puts the boy's body on his own bed, stretches himself out on the child three times, and prays. The child comes to life again (1 Kgs 17:17–24).

Elisha is faced with a very similar situation, the death of the only son of a couple he knows, who had previously been infertile until he healed that problem. Now that son has died, and the parents call for Elisha. He comes and performs the same ritual that

1. Magesa, *African Religion*, 216–18.

Elijah had, stretching himself on the child, mouth to mouth, eyes to eyes, hands to hands, seven times, until the child finally revives (2 Kgs 4:1–37). Although the suggestion is that these prophets are transferring life from themselves into the boys, they need to do this by physically replicating the position of the dead boys; they symbolically shared the death, or "carried" it, in order to produce life.

Biomedicine approaches disease differently. In the same way that it has separated itself from nature or God, and separated the control of symptoms from the roots of disease, it has also separated the techniques of symptom control from the one employing them. The healer in biomedicine does not need to have experienced a disease in order to treat it effectively; we even prefer our healers to be "healthy" in order to set good examples.

Any compassion that a physician shows—any comforting touch, any supportive listening, any tears shed—while appreciated, is completely outside the realm of biomedicine: it cannot be studied in a randomized, controlled trial. The practitioner of biomedicine does not try to carry a disease but to eliminate it.

## Excerpt in Poetry

In 1943, well into the biomedical paradigm, but long before today's hubris, T. S. Eliot published *Four Quartets*, which contains these lines:

> The wounded surgeon plies the steel
> That questions the distempered part;
> Beneath the bleeding hands we feel
> The sharp compassion of the healer's art
> Resolving the enigma of the fever chart.
>
> Our only health is the disease
> If we obey the dying nurse
> Whose constant care is not to please
> But to remind of our, and Adam's curse,
> And that, to be restored, our sickness must grow worse.[2]

2. Eliot, *Four Quartets*, "East Coker," IV.

What does this mean? Is there a profound truth here, or is Eliot just playing with us with his paradoxes? In choosing biomedicine as a metaphor to say something about the human condition, is he also saying something about biomedicine itself? Why is the surgeon wounded? Why is the nurse dying?

On one level, of course, this could be a picture of the crucified Savior. Years after the Eliot poem, Henri Nouwen, drawing from this understanding of a crucified Savior, developed the theme of the wounded healer, suggesting that it is only when we confront our own brokenness that we can effectively be present for, and possibly help heal, someone else's brokenness.[3] The obvious applications of this insight are with psychological and spiritual brokenness.

Eliot's description of a surgeon with bleeding hands wielding a scalpel, and a dying nurse ensuring that our sickness gets worse seem to show the folly of applying the theme of the wounded healer to biomedicine. Trying to spiritualize biomedicine will only reduce its effectiveness; better it remain only a technique, and the wounded surgeon be only the crucified Savior.

This seems to be common sense, but we should not excuse biomedicine so readily. Biomedicine is today, for many Americans, the only source of healing care. If Matthew is correct and disease must be carried, and if biomedical practitioners cannot carry disease, then how can people who depend only on biomedicine be healed?

Since poetry helped us ask the question, we will turn to fiction to begin to address it. In Charles Williams's 1937 novel *Descent into Hell*, a young woman bothered by a sense that there is someone or something constantly following her, dogging her footsteps; something like a ghost, but a ghost of herself. Another character (in a chapter titled "The Doctrine of Substituted Love") offers to carry for her the fear of this ghost, an idea she finds nonsensical because she cannot understand how someone can carry someone else's fear.

The helping character does not explain how except in very physical terms: if I carry a package for you, you no longer feel the

3. See Nouwen, *The Wounded Healer*.

weight of it. But is it right, she asks, to push your burdens onto someone else? Not if you choose to be completely autonomous and make a universe for yourself, he answers. "But if you will be part of the best of us, and live and laugh and be ashamed with us, then you must be content to be helped."[4] She agrees; he carries the fear, and she is free of it.

This is a fictional illustration of what we suggested in Chapter 3, that because we are part of something else, something bigger, than our own bio-life, then we cannot be autonomously ill. Likewise, we cannot be autonomously healed. Manipulating the biomechanics of disease is not enough.

From poetry and fiction, then, we can get some glimpses of what this all might mean in theology and psychology. But what about biomedicine? More directly, have we in biomedicine ever asked what it might mean for us to carry someone's *disease*? Does the question even make any sense? Let us pursue both answers— that the question makes no sense, or that it does make sense.

## Removing Disease

Possibly it does not make sense to ask practitioners of biomedicine to try to carry the diseases of their patients. Perhaps relieving or removing the disease—the stated aim of biomedicine—is sufficient. What can be wrong with that? Look at Illich's *Medical Nemesis*. The central thesis of that book is that modern biomedicine—the biomedicine that mechanically removes disease without carrying it—also removes a person's cultural and spiritual ability to bear the parts of the disease that cannot be removed.

"Culture makes pain tolerable by interpreting its necessity; only pain perceived as curable is intolerable."[5] Unfortunately, in this age of "medical miracles," all pain in Western cultures is perceived as curable; consequently, all pain is intolerable. Our jails are full of people who have tried to relieve pain with illegal drugs;

4. Williams, *Descent*, 99.
5. Illich, *Medical Nemesis*, 134.

our homes are full of people who leave with new prescriptions after every encounter with a doctor. This medicalization, instead of making us feel healthier, makes *all* aches and pains intolerable. No one has lifted and received our infirmities; no one has carried our diseases. The consequence of not asking biomedical practitioners to try to carry our patients' disease boomerangs back to us as patients with even more disease.

## Carrying Disease

Following the other argument—that it does make sense to ask doctors and nurses to carry disease—is no easier. If not carrying disease leads to medical nemesis and more disease, carrying disease leads to the wounded surgeon plying the steel, and to the dying nurse; it leads to the cross. This is not a technique that can be taught to doctors in training; this is not "communication skills" or "supportive psychotherapy." This, in fact, has little to do with biomedicine.

Let biomedicine work on the mechanics of bio-life; carrying disease brings us around to the Suffering Servant who carried our infirmities and to the Author of Life. "In the Christian tradition," Illich says, "we hope to receive this Life as a gift; and we hope to share it. We know that this Life was given to us on the Cross and we cannot seek it except on the *via crucis*."[6] We also cannot pretend to carry disease in any other way.

We biomedicine practitioners are confronted with two paradoxes. When we sidestep carrying disease, our biomedical treatment produces more suffering; yet when we don't sidestep it, carrying disease involves suffering. There is no choice free of suffering; our choice is whether we subject our patients to the risk of more suffering because of how we treat them, or subject ourselves to the risk of suffering by choosing to carry their diseases.

6. Illich, *Brave New Biocracy*.

We cannot avoid, what Michael Kelly Blanchard calls in one of his songs "the holy land of the broken heart."[7]

The problem of subjecting out patients or ourselves to the risk of more suffering, however, is not the dilemma it first appears to be if we understand the literal meaning of suffering. The *fer* at the end of the word *suffer* means "to bear or carry," as in *ferry* or *transfer*, and the *su* at the beginning of *suffer* is from *sub*, or *under*. To suffer is simply to carry, or bear under ("sub-fer") affliction. Suffering is *how* we live with affliction, not the affliction itself. Affliction is an evil we want to relieve; suffering is a culturally and spiritually determined gift we need to enhance. This is why we can pray to be kept in the holy land of the broken heart.

It is difficult to find examples of biomedical practitioners anywhere "carrying disease," especially in the middle of busy hospitals where the focus is on up-to-date technology delivered efficiently and expertly. Sometimes we need to see biomedicine practiced outside of Western culture to begin to think of how we could do things differently—better even—in the West. A young American doctor and anthropologist on her first trip to Rwanda observed Rwandan doctors at work, especially as they treated distraught patients jolted into memories of the genocide by a memorial service the night before. She recorded this in her journal:

> [They] treat their patients with such LOVE. I had noticed it before today and actually thought consciously about it, about how it wasn't just warmth and respect and consideration they show—it's really love. Then today, we had a conversation about it . . . . [One doctor] said you have to love your patients; [another] told us that in Kinyarwandi, there is no word for like, they only have a word for love. And that in medical school here, they are taught that they have to love their patients and marry their disease. To me as a doctor, that sounds CRAZY!!! Marry my patients' diseases???[8]

7. Blanchard, "The Holy Land of the Broken Heart" (also called "The Hope That Ends the Human Drought"), track 4 on Blanchard, *Mercy in the Maze*.

8. Arbour, journal entry for April 13, 2007, shared in a personal

The young American's incredulity is a sensible response for a practitioner of pure biomedicine, but the argument of this book is that pure biomedicine is not enough.

## Learning to Suffer

Looking again, then, at the two paradoxes above, we can more accurately say (à la Illich) that biomedicine often produces more *affliction*; we can only hope our patients are able to bear it, to suffer. On the other hand, the way of the cross *is* the way of suffering, the way of carrying, of "marrying" disease.

Can we learn to suffer? I hope so, and two streams of thought may help us enter the question. The first concerns the paschal mystery; the second, community.

The paschal mystery in the Catholic tradition is the fleshing out of John 12:24: "Unless a grain of wheat falls on the ground and dies, it remains only a single grain; but if it dies, it yields a rich harvest." This is beautifully explained by Ronald Rolheiser in *The Holy Longing*,[9] and provides an appropriate coda for our Death and Life chapter 2.

Rolheiser names two kinds of death: Terminal death is simply the end of life. Paschal death, however, is the end of one kind of life in preparation for receiving a richer life. He also proposes two kinds of life: "resuscitated life"—a reversal of terminal death that restores the original life; and "resurrected life," not the restoration of the previous life, but the reception of a radically new life. Lazarus was resuscitated; Jesus resurrected. The paschal mystery concerns paschal death and resurrection.

The suffering of the *via crucis* is the paschal mystery. I cannot carry my own affliction, or someone else's, by simply hoisting it up and lugging it around with me. Or rather, I can try to carry affliction that way, but eventually I will tire, or resent it, or absorb the burden so much that I become diseased. Paschal suffering is

communication with the author.

9. Rolheiser, *Holy Longing*, 141–66.

not accomplished by Herculean strength; the precursor is not a spiritual workout making me less vulnerable to being exhausted, angry, or sick.

Paschal suffering means paschal death. I must die to the desire not to be bothered by the affliction; I must die to the fear that the affliction will overwhelm me; I must die to the hope for hero status because I've carried so much. And as I die those deaths, I can look forward not to a resuscitation of who I was, but to a resurrected life, a radically new life. I will be different, richer, precisely because I have suffered. Far from being something we need to "relieve," and more than simply something we must put up with, suffering becomes the means by which we receive new life; it produces in us patience, perseverance, and hope (Rom 5:3–4).

## Suffering in Community

The other reminder that helps us enter suffering is the reality of community. No one needs to carry trouble alone, to be alone. When we are dying paschal deaths, we can feel the same way we do confronting bio-death; the pain can be as acute. We need each other. Possibly the best way to see this is with a story.

Several years ago the anesthetist from a hospital where I worked in Africa committed suicide. He had extraordinary skills and unusual dedication. We were all shocked when he took his own life; we knew he had financial and marital difficulties but did not know how serious they were.

At the funeral, just after the burial, a Kenyan surgeon who had worked closely with him came up to my wife and me. It was hot; there were no trees to stand under next to the fresh mound of earth over the body. It was the first time we had seen this surgeon since the anesthetist's death. He told us, "I've been trying to avoid him since I heard that he died . . .Sometimes I feel like—did I let him down? He came to me for money; I didn't have much money; I gave him a little." We talked it through, sharing stories, wondering what it all meant. And then he told us something that stuck with me: "I think he didn't remember he was not alone. There were other people around. Once you think you are alone in the wilderness . . . Ah . . ." And again: "He forgot at one moment that he was not alone. He thought he was alone."

It was a silhouette, an outline of a dazzling truth that the anesthetist was momentarily blinded to by his troubles. *No one,* the surgeon was saying, is alone—a truth that many Africans still remembers in crowded buses and on streets packed with people walking, talking, and laughing together, while we in the West watch this truth slip away. We know it has to be true, this business of not being alone, and we try to hold on to it in our religions and our online communities and our support groups and our counseling . . . and all of these attempts are just more evidence that true community is slipping away, and that we are more and more alone—alone in our cars in a traffic jam, alone playing solitaire with a computer.

And so we come to the end of the argument. Healing is wholeness, disease is fragmentation, disintegration,[10] disembodiment. The power of God can restore wholeness; the power of biomedicine tries to repair the diseased fragments but cannot reunite them. The hand of biomedicine holds the scalpel, the X-ray, the evidence, and the power to heal fatal wounds; it remains a closed fist. The hand that would restore life is open, empty, and pierced.

10. Berry, *Membership,* 90.

# Part Four

## Conclusion

The picture shows Christ, just taken down from the cross . . . In the picture, the face is terribly mangled by blows, swollen, with terrible, swollen, bloody bruises, the eyes open and unfocused; the whites wide open, gleaming with a kind of deathly, glazed lustre . . . If a corpse like that (and it must certainly have been exactly like that) was seen by all his disciples, his future chief apostles, and seen by the women who followed him and stood by the cross, by in fact all who believed in and worshipped him, how could they have believed, looking at such a corpse, that the martyr would rise again?

—FYODOR DOSTOEVSKY, *THE IDIOT*, 1868

Used to be sort of high and mighty, sort of priests, those doctors and lawyers and all, but they're beginning to look more and more like mechanics.

—KURT VONNEGUT JR., *PLAYER PIANO*, 1952

# 9

# Metaphors

I WONDER WHAT SUSAN Sontag would have thought of the suggestion in the Preface that my mother's mutism was a metaphor. In
her books *Illness as Metaphor* and *AIDS and Its Metaphors*,[1] now
published together, Sontag says on the very first page, "My point is
that illness is *not* a metaphor," and throughout the book she uses
the phrase "just a disease" to indicate how she thinks we ought to
look at all diseases. These books together employ a wide-ranging
definition of metaphor, encompassing stereotype, myth, fantasy,
superstition, popular imagination, stigma, and discredited beliefs
about certain diseases, especially tuberculosis, cancer, and AIDS.
The point of this well-written foray into history and literature is to
show how damaging these falsehoods can be to the one with the
disease.

Sontag is of course right when she exposes and corrects falsehoods about disease causation. However, her aim is not only to
remove false "meanings" of disease, but all meaning. The purpose
of her writing, she says, is "not to confer meaning ... but to deprive
something of meaning." In challenging the hurtful and wrong
metaphors surrounding disease, she challenges all metaphors.
She wants to remove damaging myths and stigma *so that* people
will seek proper and early biomedical treatment, betraying a

1. Sontag, *Illness as Metaphor*, 3, 102.

confidence and faith in my profession far beyond the confidence I have in it. She implies that a biomedical correction of the mechanics of disease is sufficient, a contention we challenged in Chapter 6.

To be sure, disease metaphors have two related problems. We can get the metaphor wrong—the fever of tuberculosis used to represent the inward burning of artistic passion—and we can apply this wrong metaphor to the persons infected, suggesting *their* artistic passion caused *their* tuberculosis. Sontag disabuses us of these wrong notions and similar ones surrounding cancer and AIDS.

However, the Gospel writers frequently employ diseases as metaphors for the larger story they are trying to tell. Jesus warns his followers about being too quick to impute meaning, especially wrong meaning, to disease, as when Jesus refuses to identify sin as the reason for a man's congenital blindness (John 9:3). But many— perhaps all—of Jesus' healing miracles seem to echo or illustrate the teachings or events in the Gospels. Reading the Bible without thinking metaphorically drastically limits our comprehension of it.

## Biblical Metaphors

Look again, for example, at the story of Zechariah and Elizabeth, the parents of John the Baptist (Luke 1:5–25). The major healing in this story is the cure of their infertility, and their son is described as a symbol of, or metaphor for, Elijah. But there is another part of this story that we haven't previously considered. When Zechariah questions the prophecy of Gabriel that he and Elizabeth will become pregnant in their old age, Gabriel tells Zechariah that he will lose his power of speech until the child is born. This audience with Gabriel is in the temple, and when Zechariah comes out he is mute and remains mute until John is born and circumcised (1:59–66) .

Mutism in the Gospels is usually a "spiritual" issue. The only "purely physical" healing of speech is in Mark (7:31–37), and the problem there is called a speech impediment likely related to congenital deafness, not pure mutism. All the other instances of mutes being healed (Matt 9:32–34, 12:22–23; Mark 9:14–29) mention demon-possession. When Zechariah comes out of the temple after a long time and is unable to speak, the people do not immediately assume he had had a stroke; they know he has received a vision (Luke 1:21–22). It seems that not being able to talk, especially in Zechariah's case, is a metaphor for something.

Clearly, not being able to talk after having talked for many years is an unusual, bizarre situation. As I suggested in the Preface, talking is one of the ways we connect to the world. We know and are known by conversation. If I can't walk, you can still interact with me; if I can't see, you can still perceive what my personality is. But if I can't talk, you don't know me; you don't know how to relate to me. None of the blind people in the Gospels are said to be demon-possessed; most of the mute people are. Talking is more than a matter of a properly functioning larynx and tongue.

We have one small clue about the meaning of Zechariah's muteness. The angel Gabriel tells him that he, Gabriel, had been "sent to speak to you" (Luke 1:19 RSV), and since Zechariah does not believe him, he will for a time be "unable to speak" (Luke 1:20 RSV). Gabriel begins a conversation, but Zechariah is slow to join that conversation except with doubt. The consequence is that his choice to not join the conversation is confirmed; his temporary muteness is a metaphor for his own reluctance to engage with Gabriel and his message.

For nine months his faith, like his son, gestates. Then on the day of the circumcision Zechariah is asked what his son's name should be, and he writes on a tablet the name John, which also becomes his doxology: John means "Yahweh is gracious." Zechariah regains his power of speech and praises God, rejoining the conversation Gabriel had initiated (Luke 1:59–66).

## The Broken Bread

Possibly the most obvious place where healing miracles are also metaphors follows the feeding of the five thousand. This is the only miracle other than the resurrection that is recorded in all four Gospels (Matt 14:13–21; Mark 6:30–44; Luke 9:10–17; John 6:1–15). It is at the center of Matthew, the "balanced" Gospel, and keeps coming up throughout the three middle chapters of Mark (6–8). It is mirrored in another miracle, the feeding of the four thousand (Matt 15:32–39; Mark 8:1–10), and is the starting point for Jesus' well-known Bread of Life sermon in John 6 (vv. 22–59). It is clearly a pivotal event for the writers of all of the Gospels. And both large-scale feedings follow large-scale healings, though these aren't the healings that are distinctively metaphorical.

Shortly before the miraculous feeding, Jesus sends out his twelve disciples two by two to heal the sick, cast out demons, and preach that the kingdom of heaven is "near" (Matt 10:5–15, especially v. 7; Mark 6:6–13; Luke 9:1–6). When they return, Jesus suggests they go on a retreat to rest (Mark 6:45–46; Luke 9:10). Besides this, Jesus has just heard the news of the death of his cousin, John the Baptist; he also needs a retreat (for this sequence of events, see Mark 6).

However, when they arrive at their quiet, remote place, they find a crowd of over five thousand people have followed them there. After Jesus has taught them and healed their sick, the disciples, mentally prepared for a retreat, suggest that he send the crowd away. Jesus, mentally prepared for a lesson, suggests that they feed the crowd, a task far grander than the preaching or healing they were used to. They protest but finally find a boy with a lunch: five bread loaves and two small fish (Matt 14:13–17; Mark 6:34–38; Luke 9:11–13; John 6:1–9). Jesus takes the bread and fish, thanks God, breaks the bread and distributes it, and feeds everyone there, with twelve baskets of leftovers (Matt 14:18–21; Mark 6:39–44; Luke 9:14–17; John 6:10–14).

Then Jesus goes to the mountain to pray while the disciples head home by boat. They are confused: they are deprived of their promised rest, worn out by rowing against the wind, and have no idea what the miracle they have just seen means. Then Jesus walks out to them on the lake, utterly frightening them by his ghost-like arrival (Matt 14:22–27; Mark 6:45–52).

A short time later there is the feeding of the four thousand, also following the healings of many disabled people—blind, lame, mute, and others. It's a similar story to the five thousand, except that there are seven loaves, a few small fish, and seven baskets of leftovers (Matt 15:32–39; Mark 8:1–10). In fact the similarities to the first feeding are so close, they are comical. When Jesus suggests feeding the four thousand, the disciples raise the same protest they had the first time around: where can they get bread in such a remote place? It seems they not only failed to understand the first feeding, they also forgot it.

Just after this, in another boat scene, Jesus begins to bring things to a head. When the five thousand are fed, he asks, how many baskets were left over? And after the four thousand? The disciples give the right answers. But then, apparently without helping them to understand, Jesus asks, Do you still not understand? Do you have eyes but don't see, and ears but can't hear? (Matt 16:5–12; Mark 8:14:21).

These questions introduce the metaphorical but also very real healing of the blind man at Bethsaida, the healing that comes in two stages (Mark 8:22–26). Jesus touches his eyes with spittle, causing him to see just the outlines of people walking around, as if they are trees (vv. 22–24). Then Jesus touches his eyes again, and he sees clearly (vv. 25–26). And just before the feeding of four thousand, Mark had foreshadowed the whole discussion with the account of Jesus healing the deaf, speech-impaired man—another metaphorical, and very real, healing (Mark 7:31–37).

Now it is time for Jesus to open the eyes and ears of the disciples. It all centers, he suggests, on who he really is, which is how we began our reading of the healing miracles in Chapter 3. Only now it is Peter, not one of the demons, who declares that Jesus is the promised Messiah, the Anointed One, the incarnate Christ. (Matt 16:13–17; Mark 8:27–29; Luke 9:18–20). Just as he instructed the demons, so Jesus warns his disciples to tell no one, but this time he goes on to explain that he must die (Matt 16:20–21; Mark 8:30–31; Luke 9:21–22). Peter has begun to see, but he does not yet see clearly; he begins arguing with Jesus. Jesus needs to touch his eyes again (Matt 16:22–23; Mark 8:32–33). Let me explain, Jesus seems to say, what is at the core of the incarnation, this gospel I've been teaching you.

The only way there was enough bread for the five thousand and the four thousand is that it was broken. The only way there will be enough of me, says Jesus to the disciples, is if I'm broken. And so it is with you disciples, he goes on: The only way there is enough of you to do all the healing and preaching you did on your mission, and the only way you'll be able to do it all again during your vacation when you're exhausted, is if you're broken. We are again in the Holy Land of the Broken Heart.

But, the disciples might have protested, we're trying as hard as we can! There's nobody else to do this mission, and we're so exhausted we've even burned out. And Jesus would have responded: I don't want you burned out: I want you broken. For anyone who walks in my shoes must utterly deny and disown any right to a retreat, any ownership or responsibility for a "right" way of doing things, and follow (Matt 16:24–28; Mark 8:34–38; Luke 9:23–26).

The one who saves all these things is fully and utterly destroyed, but the one who is broken to them is protected, preserved, and healed. For, Jesus says in John 6, I am the bread that helps you understand what life really is (vv. 35ff.). What I do, what I am, you must take into yourselves. The dying, yes, but also the resurrecting. I am the bread you must eat.

This is, of course, a hard saying with its overtones of cannibalism on the one hand, and brokenness and death on the other. It costs Jesus some followers—those, I think, who finally understood what this broken bread was all about. They were willing to work hard and even burn out, but they could not risk utterly losing themselves (John 6:60–66). Some things are too precious to let go of. We'll give our lives to a cause and work till we drop helping other people—as long as we remain in control of the giving and working. We'll combat world hunger and disease as long as we never have to experience it.

These stories are at the center of all the Gospels because they are at the center of the gospel. Jesus feeds over nine thousand people not to combat world hunger and disease, but to show with bread and fish and puzzling questions and healings the essence of his incarnation. It is real bread and real fish that fed people, in the same way that God really became human in Jesus. And in order for that real bread and fish to feed everyone, it had to be broken.

But the incarnation is not only Jesus' story. Jesus suggests in these stories that the incarnation is for his followers as well. As we said in the last chapter, we—including we who practice biomedical healing—serve best by becoming part of the people we are serving, by becoming incarnate in that sick community, as Jesus did. Somehow, sharing their problems is more important than fixing them. And in becoming members of that community of people needing healing, we lose some control over how we want to fix it. We become like the bread: not stretched and torn apart by the people we're trying to serve, but broken and blessed by God.

The metaphor for curing blindness and deafness is explicit in these healings. The metaphoric meaning of some of the other healings, however, is not as clearly stated. With his parables, Jesus explains a few and leaves us to puzzle over what the others mean. Perhaps we are meant to do the same with the miracles: to take a clue from those with obvious metaphorical meanings and to puzzle over what metaphorical meanings the other healings might have. And as with the parables, interpreting them represents not an exercise to find the "right" meaning, but an exercise to help us approach the heart of God.

Look, for example, at the healing of the man with the dried up or "withered" hand (Matt 12:9–14; Mark 3:1–6; Luke 6:6–11), which we examined in Chapter 7. We suggested there that the Pharisees had taken the gift of the Sabbath and dried it up, making it into a useless obligation—much like the man's dried up right hand. But there is also an interesting parallel to a story in the book of Zechariah. There (in chapter 11) we read about shepherds who are not taking care of their sheep, and the "shepherds" clearly refer to Jewish leaders. The consequence of this neglect, according to Zechariah's prophecy, is that the worthless shepherd will be blinded in the right eye, and his arm totally withered (v. 17).

Clearly in the time of Jesus the Pharisees are the leaders who were neglecting their flock; they are metaphorically blind, with useless hands. In this healing miracle of the withered hand, the Gospel writers present the Pharisees with a picture of themselves, and then demonstrate Jesus' power to heal even their withered caretaking. It is quite possible that the Pharisees understand this metaphor very well; Luke tells us that after the healing, they are filled with rage (6:11).

## Healing as Metaphor

In the Gospel of John we see some of the metaphors, or at least the spiritual meanings, of the healing miracles described most explicitly. We have already mentioned three of them: the man paralyzed for thirty-eight years (5:1–14), the man blind from birth (9:1–12), and Lazarus (11:1–44). Let us look again these stories to see how John draws the parallels between the physical healings and the spiritual meanings, thereby proclaiming the metaphorical meanings.

In John 5, there is a man paralyzed for thirty-eight years. After some preliminary conversation, Jesus tells him to "get up" or arise (v. 8). Just a few verses later, in Jesus' lengthy explanation to the Pharisees of what he was doing, he tells them that God raises the dead (v. 21); the Greek word for "get up" and "raises" is the same. The healing of the man's paralysis is clearly physical; the context of the comments about God raising the dead suggest a spiritual meaning. In the same way that Jesus healed physical paralysis, God heals spiritual paralysis.

A similar explicit parallel appears in the healing of the man born blind in John 9. The healing itself is very simple: Jesus makes some mud with his spittle, puts it on the man's eyes, and tells him to wash it off in the Pool of Siloam (vv. 6–7). But the discussion generated by the healing is long, involved, and complicated. In explaining this physical healing to the Pharisees, Jesus tells them that he has come so that those without sight might see, and those with sight might become blind (vv. 39–41). Again, Jesus is making the metaphor of the healing obvious, and is clearly talking about spiritual blindness—and once again, the Pharisees understand that he is aiming his comments at them.

The use of spittle bears comment. In the two healings we discussed above that accompanied the feeding of the four thousand, Jesus also uses spittle (see Mark 8:22–26). Why spittle? One window to understanding the meaning of spittle in first-century Palestine is to see how contemporary cultures not under the sway of biomedical reductionism view it. In many African cultures, the essence of life, or the "vital force," is felt to be concentrated in certain parts of the body, such as blood and hair. "Saliva is also perceived to have a high concentration of the life force, thus its frequent use in blessings or curses."[2] Since spittle contained power, that power could be used to heal, as in healing blindness, or to curse, as when Jesus is spat upon at his trial. Spittle comes from *inside* a person, from their core. It makes complete metaphoric sense that Jesus would use what was in his core to heal, and that his mockers would use what was in their core to curse him.

Finally, here a brief and obvious note about Lazarus. When Jesus arrives at Bethany and finds that Lazarus has already died, Martha chastises him for not coming earlier (John 11:17–22). This time, Jesus makes clear the spiritual (or metaphorical) meaning of his resuscitation before it even happens. His statement to Martha "I am the resurrection and the life" (v. 25) is a theological statement, but it also foreshadows, or predicts, the raising of Lazarus. In terms of the paschal mystery we looked at in the last chapter, Lazarus was "only" resuscitated. Jesus' statement about resurrection and life in John 11:25, however, shows us that Lazarus's resuscitated life is a metaphor for Jesus' resurrected life. That resurrection, which we will consider in the next chapter, is really the final healing miracle in the Gospels, not the repair of Malchus's ear.

Susan Sontag wanted us to eliminate metaphors from our thinking about illness and healing; the biblical stories are replete with metaphors and cannot be fully understood without resorting to them. What about biomedicine? At first, biomedicine would

---

2. Magesa, *African Religion*, 163.

seem to be free of metaphoric thinking: biomedicine is science; it deals with information and reproducible facts; there is no need to consider what it is "like unto." How we *imagine* powerful drugs or complicated surgery working will not, we think, influence how they actually work—except in the placebo effect. Metaphors may help in "patient education" and symptom relief, but not in developing a cure for cancer.

However, biomedicine is not as free of metaphors as we might think. Consider the lay term *painkiller*; consider that doctors regularly refer to the drugs available to them as their "therapeutic armamentarium." It is not difficult to build a case that modern biomedicine often functions according to a military paradigm. In the last pages of her book on metaphors, Sontag confronts this directly, writing that while "not all metaphors applied to illnesses and their treatments are equally unsavory," the one she was "most eager to see retired . . . is the military metaphor."[3] What is wrong with a military metaphor? Don't we want to "fight" disease, "kill" germs, and "conquer" cancer?

The problem with the military metaphor, especially in America, is that biomedicine follows the metaphor too closely, falling into the same pitfalls, traps, and excesses that the military does. (And yes, it is biomedicine, existing now for only about a century, which is *following* the military, which has been active for millennia.) Showing the correspondence between the two, Sontag says "the medical model of the public weal [following the military metaphor] not only provides a persuasive justification for authoritarian rule but implicitly suggests the necessity of state-sponsored repression and violence (the equivalent of surgical removal or chemical control of the offending or "unhealthy" parts of the body politic). . . It overmobilizes, it overdescribes."[4] The military paradigm has influenced how we approach healing—but in the wrong ways.

3. Sontag, *Illness as Metaphor*, 182.
4. Sontag, *Illness as Metaphor*, 182.

## Medicine and the Military

In at least three ways biomedicine, like the military, "gets it wrong"—and these wrong ways all stem from playing God. And since I came of age during the war in Vietnam and wrote the first edition of this book during the war in Iraq, those wars provide me with ready illustrations for the parallels between my profession and the military. The Iraq war also provides us with this eerie proof of the metaphor in action: Donald Rumsfeld, one of the architects of the Iraq war, spent a decade as chief executive officer of a giant pharmaceutical firm (G. D. Searle) between his terms as defense secretary under presidents Ford and Bush.

First, we suggested in Chapter 6 that biomedicine had to ignore the true origins and causes of disease, and focus only on the mechanisms or on symptoms. The military, from whom biomedicine "learned" how to function, often does the same. America has been engaged in a war on terrorism for nearly twenty years; during Vietnam we were engaged in a war against communism. In the 1960s and '70s there was little government debate on why people in Southeast Asia were choosing communism; today there is a parallel lack of official debate over why people choose terrorism.

Even if the American government openly engaged those debates and uncovered the disenfranchisement, the political despair, and the poverty that often underlie the choices for communism then or terrorism now, there is very little the military could do to address those problems. The same is true if America were to confront the role it plays as a neocolonial superpower in adding to that disenfranchisement: again, there is little the military could do to correct this. The military, like biomedicine, attacks symptoms. Their understanding of the problems *they* cause is very narrow—as narrow as "just" iatrogenic disease or death from "friendly fire." They seem unable to engage with the deeper problems they help create.

Second, as we proposed in Chapter 8, when biomedicine vigorously tries to remove all pain, it ends up making things worse, diminishing people's ability to carry the pain that can't be removed.

This focus on dealing only with symptoms follows directly from the inability just mentioned to address causes, and is equally true in the military. In Vietnam because we were unable to eliminate communism, we tried to kill all Viet Cong and to napalm the villages that harbored them. We failed, and as a result Vietnam survived.

In Iraq and Afghanistan, we thought the way to eliminate terrorism was to kill all terrorists and to bomb the mosques that harbor them. So far, we have made things much worse. In biomedicine we treat the pain or the excess body fluid or the tumor tissue *as* the main problems and try to remove them, even—or especially—when we can't remove the causes. In Iraq we chase down the suicide bombers and their support groups, even—or especially—when we won't remove the reasons they have become or continue to support suicide bombers.

Third, our contention in Chapter 5 was that, even though biomedicine cannot deal with root causes, it still tries to control, or at least manipulate, the future. In Vietnam, America chose a president to build the future of "South" Vietnam, one far less popular than Ho Chi Minh. America lost that war and failed to eliminate communism, but somehow communism still collapsed, likely under its own weight.

In Iraq, America still imagines it can impose its will and control the future of the Middle East, yet efforts to rebuild Middle Eastern countries, which our military helped to destroy, continue to fail.

Are biomedicine's efforts to control the future any more successful? We can control the future of a dying body for days or weeks in an intensive care unit, but is the person in intensive care better off? We are attempting to control the future of our entire population with preventive medicine, statistically adding to our lives months or years, but at the cost of making everyone a patient. Will we also attempt to control the future of our race with genetic engineering? We in biomedicine have learned our methods from the military; will we also learn from the military the cost of this approach, that war cannot bring peace, and medicine cannot bring health?

## The Meaning of Spittle

The problem is not metaphors; the problem is using the wrong ones. The military ("the armed forces") by definition uses force to solve problems; it is a logical and appropriate metaphor to illustrate anything that depends for its success on power. The Gospels, on the other hand, are replete with agricultural metaphors: with sheep and goats, with seed being sown, with vineyards being cared for and trees being pruned. They are metaphors of growth, not power. But they are not purely "natural" metaphors; people prepare the ground, sow the seed, fertilize the vines, cut the branches, and shepherd the sheep.

Human activity should not force nature; it should assist nature. Healing, being made whole, requires power (or at least activity), but it cannot be forced. As we saw in Part 2, Jesus demonstrates the power of God over death, and in Part 3 the power of God for healing. But he never forces himself on people. Sontag is right about this: the military metaphor is precisely the wrong one for healing.

Now look again at the metaphor of using spittle in healing. We suggested above that since saliva has a high concentration of the life force and comes from inside a person, it was appropriate for Jesus to use as he healed. Interestingly, it is the only "medicine" he uses. Most of the time he speaks to people, and they are healed; about half the time he also touches them. Three times he uses spittle (Mark 7:32–35, 8:22–26; John 9:6–7). In these cases Jesus himself is the medicine.

In *Biohealth*, the sequel to the first edition of this book, I discuss influence of the profit-driven pharmaceutical industry in determining how we go about our work of healing, especially as it focuses our attention on its products, and away from other ways of healing. Like military metaphors, the pharmaceutical industry drives how biomedicine conceives of healing. It tells us that medicines are necessary, that without them (to control a disease, kill a bacterium, force the body back into balance) we cannot heal. We, doctors as well as patients, have internalized this belief; there is no treatment without an injection, a prescription, or a procedure.

Jesus modeled another kind of healing, which, according to the Gospels, possessed considerable power. He listened to people's pleas, he spoke to them, he touched them, and he sometimes gave them something from the very essence of himself—his spittle. Should we do any less?

# Chapter 10

# Resurrection and Renunciation

A STORY WITH METAPHORIC meaning is not always literally true. Consider resurrection. Resurrection themes are common in human experience, possibly because we all confront death, often before we are ready for it. Resurrection metaphors—reincarnation in some eastern religions, Quetzalcoatl for the Aztecs, Osiris for the Egyptians, spring following winter in temperate climates—bespeak hope.

What we lost, we hope, does not cease to exist. We hold on to memories, and the metaphors that sustain them, in order to resist or hoodwink or sidestep death, to deny it its final power, to affirm it is not the end. Even when we fail to defeat death, our metaphors tell us that some kind of life goes on.

Admittedly not all metaphors lack literal meaning. In temperate climates, spring really does follow winter; leafless trees that appear to be dead suddenly bloom. It is no surprise that European Christianity was comfortable with Easter in their spring. It is such an appropriate fit that in secular America we sometimes conflate the two; Easter *is* spring—and then the resurrection of Christ, like Quetzalcoatl and Osiris, becomes *only* a metaphor.

In contrast, many believe that Christ was literally resurrected, but they are sometimes content to consign that event only to history, see it as a proof that Jesus really was divine, and . . . and what? It was the crucifixion that dealt with sin, but what do we do with the resurrection? Hymenaeus and Philetus, in Saint Paul's time, did not deny the resurrection; they simply felt that it had already taken place—and Paul says they had missed the truth (2 Tim 2:17–18).

It could be that Hymenaeus and Philetus represent many in pious America today (the exact opposite of secular America): they saw resurrection as *only* literal, an event that had already taken place, but an event that could not be repeated and had no ongoing, metaphoric meaning. The richness of the gospel story is that Christ's resurrection, the last healing miracle in the Gospels, is both literal and metaphoric. We conclude with a look at this healing.

## The Resurrection in History

The events as the separate gospels record them are familiar. Jesus is one of three men killed in a public execution in Jerusalem (Matt 27:38; Luke 23:32; John 19:18) and is the first of the three to die (Mark 15:44; John 19:31–35). The same day he dies, he is wrapped in a shroud and buried in a tomb hewn out of rock (Matt 27:59–60; Mark 15:46; Luke 23:50–53). Several women had prepared spices to anoint Jesus' body but delayed for a day since the day after his death was the Sabbath (Mark 15:42; Luke 23:54; John 19:42). As soon as Jewish law allowed, early the following morning, they come to the tomb to finish their burial customs (Mark 16:1; Luke 23:56—24:1; John 19:39–40). It is then that they find the empty tomb (Mark 16:5–7; Luke 24:1–3; cf. John 20:1–2) with an angel sitting on the tombstone (Matt 28:1–7).

Jesus tells them to inform the disciples (Matt 28:1–2; cf. John 20:1–17), which they do, and promptly Peter and John (John 20:3–10; cf. Luke 24:12) come to verify that the tomb is empty. The women, nevertheless, are the first to see the resurrected Jesus outside the tomb (Matt 27:8–10). Later that day he walks with the two men who do not recognize him on the road to Emmaus (Luke 24:13–32) and that evening visits most of the disciples (Luke 24:36–49; John 20:19–23). Thomas isn't there (John 20:24–25), so a week later Jesus returns for Thomas's benefit (John 20:24–29). Then a little over a month later, after several more appearances in Galilee, Jesus ascends from the Mount of Olives just outside Jerusalem (Matt 28:16–20; Luke 24:50–53; Acts 1:6–11).

But Jesus' resurrection is not only the ultimate healing of the Gospels, both literally and metaphorically. It is also what Christians claim it to be: a historical demonstration of God's power. As we saw in the resuscitation of Lazarus, that raising was a political event prompting the authorities to plan to destroy the evidence—Lazarus himself. Matthew says the same power issues were at play with Jesus' resurrection. When the guards hired by the religious leaders reported their story of the missing body, those religious leaders realized again that the power over death confers the power to name what is going on, a power they were not willing to let go of. They were ready with a spin and a cover-up; maintaining power was again more important than evidence-based truth (Matt 27:62–66; 28:11–15).

As in all the other healing miracles, we get no details about the mechanisms of this resurrection. Jesus died, and the same Jesus somehow returned to a kind of human life, which would never result in death again. And this same sort of resurrection, according to Saint Paul in 1 Cor 15, is in store for all of us. Not resuscitation, which is the best biomedicine can offer, but resurrection. What is involved in this for us? What does this mean?

The first time Jesus tells his disciples clearly that he is going to be killed (Matt 16:21–23; Mark 8:27–30; Luke 9:18–20), he also tells them that three days later he will be resurrected. They become upset about the dying part (Peter blurts out that it shouldn't happen!), but apparently don't really hear the resurrection part, and don't comment on that.

Nevertheless, Jesus takes them to the next step, and shows them some connections they hadn't asked about. First, he says, to follow him, they also must die (carry their own crosses). But more than this, the ones who try to not die will end up losing their lives, but the ones who renounce themselves and their lives will end up finding life (Matt 16:24–28; Mark 8:34–38; Luke 9:23–27) The key to resurrection, Jesus seems to be saying, is renunciation.

## Renunciation Tradition

There is a strong biblical tradition of renunciation as a way to freedom, even a foreshadowing of freedom from the restrictions and "necessities" imposed by the fall. Jacques Ellul suggests that fasting "shatters the necessity" of eating, keeping the Sabbath shatters the necessity of toil, and giving shatters the necessity of money.[1]

Fasting, of course, does not abolish the need for eating, but it metaphorically challenges the preeminence of food ("Man does not live on bread alone"). Keeping the Sabbath, as we previously discussed, causes us to remember God's creation before the fall, to metaphorically declare that work is not sovereign. Renouncing food or work or money, even for a day, denies food and work and money the power to name what is going on. Renouncing declares, as our first chapter makes clear, that our allegiance lies elsewhere.

Likewise, Jesus seems to be saying that renouncing life shatters the necessity of death. As we saw with the paschal mystery in Chapter 8, the only way to be resurrected is to first die. For us, being part of the resurrection does not involve preparing our bodies by keeping them alive as long as possible, patching them up with borrowed and artificial organs, resisting bio-death at all costs.

Bio-death—and bio-life—are not sovereign. We in the kingdom of heaven are free to renounce whatever is not sovereign. In fact, we must: to participate in the resurrection to Life, we must renounce the sovereign claims of bio-life. Indeed, the one that saves life loses it, but the one that loses life saves it.

## Our Choices

The challenge for us who live in Babylon is clear. We are awed by the power of biomedicine and have delegated to biomedicine the power to name what is going on. But biomedicine does not really have power over death; its power is only over mechanisms: it is the power of the beast whose fatal wound is healed in Rev 13:3. This is

1. Ellul, *Violence*, 128.

not a power that frees us—it is a power that enslaves us, that wants to make us all patients.

But we have choices. We can renounce these claims of bio-medicine.[2] Consider my father. He was in most respects a conventional, or even model, American citizen. He was an Eagle Scout, a World War II veteran, a devout churchgoing Christian, a devoted husband and father, a chemical engineer, and a faithful employee of the same company for over thirty years. But he never learned how to swallow pills: a most profound if unconscious rebellion against modern medical care. The first requirement of being a patient is being able to swallow pills—and our health care system tells us that we are all patients now, even we who are healthy. My father apparently disagreed. He stubbornly never learned to swallow pills in the same way that he would have stubbornly refused the 666 tattoo on his forehead had he lived in the world of Revelation (see Rev 13:16–18). He knew that he did not need to buy or sell from the beast, that he did not need the pills of biomedicine.

My father's hope was elsewhere, in Christ's historical, and his own eventual, resurrection. At age eighty-five during his final contact with biomedicine, in the emergency room, my sister clarified with him one more time the meaning of his advance directives: that he wanted nothing extraordinary done if his vital functions were to stop. He nodded. And just to make sure, she said, "That means, you might die." And that was when he broke into a grin. "Wonderful," he said, "then I'll be with the Lord."

Biomedicine will not willingly let go of the power to name what is going on. But we need not pry it loose or battle for it. We do have choices: we can renounce biomedicine altogether and immerse ourselves in some form of alternative medicine, and for some diseases we will get more succor there than from bio-medicine. Ultimately, though, we will need to confront alternative medicine's alternative claim to name what is going on—and we will need to ignore the real power of biomedicine.

There is another choice. We can selectively accept some of the powers of biomedicine and selectively renounce others, as we will

2. Illich, "Health."

suggest in the next chapter. But the key is this: whether we use the power of biomedicine or renounce it, we must in both cases deny it the power to name for us what is going on. Resurrection shows us where *that* power is. We are now back to where we started: our kingdom is not of this world. The kingdom of this world may provide us with the power to manipulate disease mechanisms; the kingdom of heaven shows us the power to name what is going on.

# Chapter 11

# Back to Biomedicine

RESURRECTION MAY BE THE end of the story—but frankly, we are not there yet. We still live with our broken, unresurrected bodies. And the elephant in the room I have not yet mentioned is that today, at the beginning of the twenty-first century, Jesus is not walking around America (or anywhere else) commanding lame people to walk, opening the eyes of congenitally blind people by touch, or calling dead people out of graves.

God is still incarnate in the body of Christ, the church—but for whatever reason, the church does not seem to have the power of Christ in literally opening the eyes of the blind, making the lame walk, or raising the dead (at least not very often, if at all). A dialogue between biblical healing and biomedicine may be interesting, but can it be anything more than interesting when we *have* biomedicine but no longer have biblical healing?

To focus this question, what have we learned by this dialogue—and specifically, how does the dialogue help us to sensibly use the biomedicine we *have* even if we don't allow it the power to name what is going on? Can the insights of biblical healing be applied to biomedicine, and if biomedicine has become utterly separate from anything spiritual, can it be redeemed?

I have my doubts. As we have seen, the power of biomedicine as a technique is intimately related to its focus on mechanisms and its autonomy from the spiritual world. The debate with biblical healing becomes important not to see who "wins" the debate, but to outline the limits of biomedical technique so that its practitioners do not expect it to perform what it cannot. When we who accept the spiritual world resist allowing biomedicine the power to name what is going on, we can more comfortably accept its power to manipulate bio-mechanisms. We can also see more clearly which parts of biomedicine are helpful and be more selective in our choices of its techniques.

Let us review for a moment the tasks that biomedicine takes on:

1) Especially in the last several decades, as we saw in Chapter 6, biomedicine has claimed expertise in *preventive medicine.* This involves manipulating bio-mechanisms when a person has an early, asymptomatic form of disease, or even manipulating risk factors before the disease has begun. Vaccines are the truest form of preventive medicine, completely preventing the disease prior to an asymptomatic form or even a risk factor.

2) Classically, the goal of any medical practitioner has been to completely eliminate a disease once it has begun. This *curative medicine* is the most gratifying for both practitioners and patients. Sometimes, as with antibiotics treating infections, the patient is left with no "residual," no scars. Other times, as with surgical cures of cancer, there is complete cure, but with residual loss of the organ affected.

3) Many conditions are troublesome, but not progressive and not fatal—most allergies, for example, or anxiety, or disabilities such as blindness and deafness. biomedicine can provide *alleviation* for these conditions, short of actually eliminating them. In this category too are the so-called nondiseases such as baldness, grey hair, skin wrinkles, normal pregnancy, menopause, undesirable nose shape, small breasts, declining libido, and so forth: normal variations related to genetics or

aging, which biomedicine by its techniques can either allevi-
ate or even "cure."

4) Finally, in Chapter 7 we considered the large and growing category of *chronic diseases*. In contrast to the group just mentioned, these are generally progressive (they get worse with
time) and are eventually fatal without treatment. And here
too there are two groups: those diseases that do not progress
as long as the patient complies with the medical regimen—
taking daily thyroid pills for under-active thyroid, for example—and diseases that slowly progress even with treatment.
This second group is by far the largest. Heart failure and em-
physema are common examples in America; diabetes, while
theoretically nonprogressive as long the patient remains on
treatment, is in fact for most Americans progressive as well.
Included here, of course, is the true palliative care offered to
patients with terminal illnesses.

## Affirmations and Reservations

Now, the power of biomedicine that we have been discussing
throughout this book is evident with each of these tasks, though
not in equal amounts. And ironically, the places where we most
celebrate the power are not necessarily the places most worthy of
our praise, as we shall see. Where can those of us who understand
spiritual realities (who live in the kingdom of this world but have
loyalty to the kingdom of heaven), where can we be comfortable
with biomedicine?

Probably the easiest task to affirm is the second, curative
medicine. In this category are some truly wonderful accomplish-
ments of biomedicine: curing bacterial infections with antibiotics,
curing some cancers with surgery or chemotherapy, repairing bone
fractures and internal injuries after major or minor trauma, and a
whole host of focused surgeries ranging from removing cataracts
in blind eyes to cesarean sections for obstructed labor. Eliminating
disease follows the pattern of the biblical healings, requiring no

chronic medication and no "follow-up" visits. Eliminating disease is the eventual goal of all patients.

We can affirm some things in the other three categories, but with more reservations than for curative medicine. With chronic diseases, both nonprogressive (the third category) and progressive (the fourth), we are confronted with people who have afflictions that do not go away, with people who are suffering. We must listen to these patients, carry their sorrows, help them to suffer, and offer what amelioration we can. Much of this is the human, compassionate care that biomedical *practitioners* offer. But can we as readily affirm the technological commodities of biomedicine in these categories?

For progressive chronic diseases, as we have already seen in Chapter 7, the chronic disease model is not as successful as we would hope. It usually works fairly well for compliant patients (for example, my family medicine professor with diabetes), but a large percentage of our patients don't comply. Yet biomedicine—the medicine of bio-mechanisms—does not feel a responsibility for how people behave. Family medicine and public health try to address individual and community behavior, but their most powerful tools are still the tools of biomedicine. We must treat patients with progressive chronic diseases, as there can be much value in understanding their story and walking with them.[1] But we also need to be honest: the benefits of our biomedical treatments, while sometimes quite significant, are at other times small and carry their own negative side effects.

Nonprogressive chronic diseases present us with a different problem. Some of these conditions are true disabilities, and the technologies to assist these people can provide great assistance: hearing aids for the deaf, audiobooks for the blind, wheelchairs for paraplegics, and so on—most not under the control of biomedical doctors. But what about the troublesome, annoying, nonfatal chronic disturbances: allergies, pains, anxiety and mild depression, musculoskeletal aches and headaches—the kind of minor ailments almost all of us get sometimes? Or the so-called nondiseases listed

1. Kleinman, *Illness Narratives*, chapter 15.

above? Biomedicine offers treatments for all of these conditions—again, with varying results. Our success is nowhere near the level of curative medicine.

Finally, there is preventive medicine, which we have already dealt with in detail in Chapter 5. And once again, we are not proposing eliminating this category altogether for those who understand spiritual realities; clearly *some* vaccinations are valuable, for example. But beyond the problems we previously outlined—the attempt to control the health of whole populations and the disembodiment that accompanies it—there is another problem with modern preventive medicine: it isn't nearly as effective as we are led to believe. The benefits of its interventions may be *statistically* significant (becoming evident when large groups of people are studied), but they are often not *clinically* significant (that is, obvious to the patient or clinician).

A recent detailed and revealing look at the limited effectiveness of biomedicine in these last two categories—chronic nonprogressive conditions and preventive medicine—is Nortin Hadler's *The Last Well Person.*[2]

In short, we can affirm much in true curative medicine but find ourselves with reservations about the other offerings of biomedicine. Curative medicine, like biblical healing, sets the patient free; the other three engage the patient in a long-term relationship of dependency on biomedicine. Curative medicine by definition always "works"; the other three—despite some remarkable successes—cannot always "deliver." Curative medicine only sometimes leaves scars; the other three offer treatments that often have side effects.

Beyond this, although medical research is constantly enlarging our knowledge of bio-mechanisms and bio-therapies, the newest and most dramatic advances are not usually in true curative medicine. Huge research projects test new preventive medicines and medicines for chronic diseases, but few new curative drugs appear. There are remarkably sophisticated new procedures for cardiac disease and organ transplantation, but none of these cure.

2. Hadler, *Last Well Person.*

A brief word is in order about the new research frontier: gene therapy. In theory, the goal of gene therapy is to be part of curative medicine: repair or replace defective genes in a person with a disease, eliminate the disease, and the patient has no further need of biomedicine. This kind of cure would be appropriate for the very small percentage of patients whose problem is solely caused by a defective gene—and if science ever succeeds, we can affirm this cure. However, early indications are that gene therapy looks instead like chronic disease care: it requires careful ongoing monitoring and is wrought with side effects. It functions more like organ transplantation than like the cure of pneumonia with antibiotics.

The other kind of gene therapy, changing the genetic makeup of germ cells (egg and sperm) of parents so their children do not get inherited diseases, falls into the category of modern preventive medicine. The techniques, at least, are modern; the concepts seem to be borrowed from an older field, eugenics.

## America and Africa

To say all of this in another way: the medicine and surgery we practice in rural Africa is mostly curative medicine—medicine and surgery that is rarely high-tech, that has been available worldwide for decades, and that was developed mostly before the 1980 watershed I proposed in *Biohealth*. The major exception is the recent introduction of ART (antiretroviral therapy) for AIDS in Africa (which is high-tech, not curative, and is now becoming widely available), and it remains to be seen how successful this will be. If our experience treating diabetes and hypertension in America is any guide, we should not be too optimistic about ART controlling AIDS in Africa.

The obvious response to this celebration of curative medicine is that it is generally more effective against the diseases often found in rural Africa (other than AIDS)—acute, infectious, traumatic, and obstetric. The diseases of America are less often infectious and mostly chronic and degenerative—the sorts of diseases that do not lend themselves easily to curative medicine. That is true but misses the point. This is not an exercise to suggest that biomedical practitioners in Africa make better choices; it is rather an attempt to further underline that biomedicine comprises both very effective therapies and less effective ones. It is to admit that some of the therapies we offer in biomedicine free people, while others tie them to the medical system. Most people in rural Africa simply cannot afford to be permanent patients tied to the medical system.

To be more direct: biomedicine, especially preventive medicine and chronic disease care, is very expensive and requires a great deal of discipline—or control. Societies rich enough to support these forms of biomedicine must find ways of promoting conformity—or adherence or compliance—with their requirements of screening and daily drug-taking. The crudest way to accomplish this is by decree, but most Western societies are not that unsophisticated—certainly not America. Although (as we have seen) adherence is far from perfect, several societal forces work synergistically to encourage the "patient role": doctors use their authority to tell patients what they "need," pharmaceutical companies reinforce this with advertising (which seems to be education-based but is really fear-based), and insurance plans validate the need for these products by paying for at least part of them.

Underneath all this, people are afraid that without these products and services they will feel discomfort, become increasingly ill, and die. We Americans, like other modern Babylonians, have internalized the need to become permanent patients tied to the medical system.

Some of us can afford this. But can the rest of the world? And does the rest of the world need *all* that we have to offer? In true curative medicine our emperor is lavishly dressed, but his garb in preventive medicine and chronic care ranges from drab to threadbare to totally absent. Yet his tailors have cleverly covered him with the latest technological "evidence"—but evidence that in good light is transparent. Consider these two representative examples:

1) Commonly used antiviral medications for influenza, while not curing the disease, do shorten the duration of illness, but

only by one day. For an illness that lasts for a week or two, how necessary is it to take an expensive drug that will produce side effects over 10 percent of the time?

2) If one hundred healthy individuals with high cholesterol take a statin drug to reduce it, three will benefit by lowered cholesterol and less risk of heart attacks. However, ninety-seven receive only side effects of, and a bill for, the medication. Maybe it does take a child to actually say, "The emperor has no clothes"!

Even though we in America don't all succeed in being "good" patients, very few of us refuse the role altogether. We could. As we showed in the last chapter, renunciation is a Christian mandate, but this is not asceticism for its own sake; we renounce something in order to get something better.

In the Christian tradition, renunciation is the door to resurrection. The Amish renounce some transportation technologies to keep their families and communities together. Nuns and monks, as we saw in the first chapter, renounce money, sex, and independence in order to bring into sharp focus some differences between the kingdom of this world and the kingdom of heaven. Might there be times when we need to renounce dependence on doctors in order to "shatter the necessity" of biomedicine? Might we even need to renounce the authority of bio-life in order to recover the value of spiritual Life? As we will see in the Afterword, Ivan Illich practiced what he preached and renounced biomedical care for himself—but never renounced Life.

Renunciation, especially renunciation of only parts of the biomedical package, is far more powerful than it first seems. Accepting all biomedicine grants it sovereignty; renouncing all of it grants to it a sort of negative sovereignty—as when we renounce or reject Satan and all his works at baptism. But when we selectively accept and selectively renounce, we strip biomedicine of its sovereignty. It returns to its creaturely status: a "power," a part of creation that is fallen. We no longer let biomedicine name for us what is going on; we no longer let it decide for us what we need.

This partial renunciation is not simply a technique; this is spiritual work. Biomedicine, we said, is a fallen principality or power. It is part of the world (*kosmos*) that God created, that fell, and that God still loves (John 3:16). But more than this, God has asked us to share in the work of reconciling this world to God (2 Cor 5:18–19). As long as biomedicine insists on remaining autonomous from anything spiritual, as I said at the beginning of this chapter, it is unlikely to be redeemed. But when we selectively renounce—dethroning biomedicine from sovereignty while accepting where it sets us free from disease—we have begun the process of reconciling it to God.

## What Hospice Teaches

There is one final reason to question the package of biomedical care we are surrounded with: a practical reason with spiritual implications. Look again specifically at biomedical care of chronic progressive diseases. When it becomes clear that our biomedical interventions are not having any effect, and the patient is in fact dying, we often change our approach and resort to palliative care, sometimes delivered in the context of hospice. With the palliative care and hospice focus, we are no longer hoping for a cure or regression of the disease.

Hospice provides relief of pain and other distressing symptoms, but in a context very different from the usual biomedical approach. Here we concentrate not on the mechanisms of disease but on the affirmation of life and the normality of death. The social, mental, and spiritual needs of the patient—there, by the way, with every disease—take center stage. We even allow people to die at home. Hospice is the one place within biomedicine where there is an open admission of the "failure" of biotechnology; biomedicine voluntarily gives up the right to name what is going on.

Unfortunately, we resort to hospice in America and other Babylons only after biomedicine has given up, and biomedicine does not easily give up. Some patients have hospice care only for the last few days of their life, or at most the last few weeks. The vast majority who benefit from hospice have cancer, even though cancer is not the only way—in fact not the most common way—that Americans die. Yet hospice encapsulates almost everything that biomedicine has lost: that life is good, that death is normal, that people are spiritual beings, and that they want help in suffering and relief of symptoms. All people with chronic progressive diseases need this kind of care, even if their death is likely decades away. It is a shame that we now associate this kind of care only with hospice, and that we have separated attempts to cure from attempts to care. All biomedical care should have a hospice attitude.

Hospice, I think, provides us with an example of how to live with the parts of biomedicine that don't cure—and even sometimes with those that do. Hospice assumes that there is a "beyond" beyond the mechanics of disease; it assumes that people are spiritual. Hospice is as comfortable with death as with life; it remembers and preserves what medicine used to be before it became biomedicine. A hospice attitude allows us to see more clearly the benefits and shortcomings of all of biomedicine because it knows biomedicine is not all there is.

# Afterword

A FEW YEARS AFTER he published *Medical Nemesis*, while in his fifties, Ivan Illich noticed a tumor growing out of the side of his face. Even as the tumor grew and caused him considerable pain, he decided not to get biomedical or surgical treatment. Over twenty years later at the age of seventy-six, he died, likely from the effects of the tumor. He wrote most of the articles I have drawn from in this book, except *Medical Nemesis* itself, while he had this tumor.

William Stringfellow, the other social critic I referred to in Chapters 2 and 4, also had a major life-threatening illness. He was in his late thirties at the time and decided to follow biomedical and surgical treatment. His surgery at around age forty was "success-ful" in preventing his impending death but left him with several chronic diseases. He died just over fifteen years later, in his middle fifties, likely from the effects of these diseases. He wrote several of his most well-known books after the surgery—and for this Af-terword the most revealing is the story of his disease, *A Second Birthday: A Personal Confrontation with Illness, Pain, and Death.*[1]

I could have said, Illich refused surgery and died from his cancer; Stringfellow accepted surgery and it saved his life. That way of speaking, however, is neither honest nor accurate. It puts surgery at the center, not the life stories of Illich and Stringfellow. It assumes biomedicine is not only pivotal but also of undisputed life-saving value. And it suggests that technology is a given that we ignore to our peril. Illich and Stringfellow incarnated for us a different approach.

1. Stringfellow, *Second Birthday.*

In Chapter 2 we suggested that whereas Stringfellow speaks of our idolatry of death, and Illich speaks of our idolatry of life, these are not really contradictory notions: both are speaking of separation from God. Likewise it may seem from their choices regarding their own diseases that Illich and Stringfellow had opposite opinions about biomedicine. Yet Stringfellow's record of his own illness reveals some striking similarities to the way Illich suffered and lived with his disease. It almost seems that Stringfellow's record applies to both men.

## William Stringfellow

In the 1960s, William Stringfellow was an activist lawyer in East Harlem; in his "spare time" he wrote books and lectured. During this time of intense activity, he admits, he became "unduly dependent upon alcohol"—until eventually his "body would no longer tolerate the stuff" and he stopped drinking completely.[2] Unfortunately he had already developed marked abdominal pain and dramatic weight loss. He was diagnosed with pancreatitis. He tried medical therapy and rest, but the pain was unrelenting; his primary doctor suggested he had a "cyst"—likely a pancreatic pseudocyst.[3] He consulted several doctors in New York City and eventually found a particularly skilled surgeon willing to operate on it.

He knew it was risky surgery; doctors then, and now, have a healthy respect for the pancreas and would prefer not to operate on it. In 1968 Stringfellow underwent a ten-hour operation involving removal of most of his pancreas, a pancreatic cyst that had nearly ruptured, and his spleen. He survived but was left with pancreatic insufficiency—which he could treat medically with replacement enzymes—and diabetes, complications of which led to his death fifteen years later.

2. Stringfellow, *Second Birthday*, 32.
3. Stringfellow, *Second Birthday*, 72.

Clearly biomedical technology played a major role in String-fellow not dying in 1968, though whether or not this technology was the sole reason for his recovery is less clear. In fact, since the surgery was so extensive and risky, his recovery was not a fore-gone conclusion: "Strange as it may seem," the surgeon reportedly told Stringfellow's waiting friends right after the procedure, "your friend is alive."[4] While Stringfellow denies that his recovery was miraculous in the sense of magical, the title of his reflections, *A Second Birthday*, betrays his belief that something extraordinary and unexpected happened. However, it is not his recovery that forms the bulk of his book, but his reflections on living with his diseases, both before and after the surgery. It is here where his writing reinforces the major themes of this book and foreshadows the suffering of Illich.

In Chapter 8 we suggested that *suffering* is not pain or af-fliction itself—it is the way we carry pain; that while pain is a symptom of spiritual death, suffering is a culturally and spiritually determined gift we should honor. Stringfellow states this in a very mundane way: "My work was my pain: my pain was my work."[5] For him, both pain and work were manifestations of the fall (Gen 3:17–19 makes this clear); both needed to be borne, to be suffered. But that work was not the work of Sisyphus, exhausting but with no results. Stringfellow "understood that the pain had become my work and that the pain represented a familiar crisis to be tran-scended by a grace also familiar. After that, though the pain did not relent, I was free of anxiety about my survival."[6]

Though Stringfellow's abdominal pain ended after his sur-gery, he was left with at least two chronic diseases which he needed to carefully manage for the rest of his bio-life. And though he was clearly grateful for that bio-life and the cessation of pain, he did not whitewash the significance of those residual diseases in his life; "If I had not crossed death's threshold, I was still not absent from the presence of death . . . Death may have been, in terms of illness,

4. Stringfellow, *Second Birthday*, 175.

5. Stringfellow, *Second Birthday*, 65.

6. Stringfellow, *Second Birthday*, 68.

foiled or cheated or detoured or put off, but the power of death had not abandoned me."[7] His description of what was required of him to treat his diabetes and pancreatic insufficiency (using phrases like "enslaved," "a chronic victim," and "the very procedures commendable for sustaining life become radically dehumanizing"[8]) should be required reading for anyone tempted to oversell the benefits of treating chronic diseases—whether diabetes or AIDS—as we suggested in Chapter 7.

In *The Politics of Spirituality*, his last book, written only a year before he died, Stringfellow returned in the Epilogue to the subject of his health. Unrelenting pain had returned, this time in his legs because of his diabetes. By now his relationship with biomedicine began to foreshadow more closely the route that Illich would take: Stringfellow tried chelation therapy—not a standard biomedical way to approach leg pain from diabetes—and refused chemical pain relievers. He also posed the sorts of questions anyone with chronic pain would pose: Why did he have such pain? Who was to blame? Was the pain a punishment? Could it be somehow edifying? And, in the middle of these questions, this one: "*Is my suffering of pain consequentially related to the massive default and multiple failures of commercialized medicine? Is pain, thus, an injustice? And in its essence more an issue of politics than of medical practice?*"[9] He suggested no answers to these queries; he could live without answers because of his belief in resurrection: "the latter day, when all of created life, myself included, gather at the throne of Judgment."[10]

But Stringfellow had already learned what it was to suffer; he knew that as pain had been his work earlier, now managing these chronic diseases and their pain was his work. And by the end of his first memoir, he could conclude—likely referring as much to his diabetes as to his surgery—"*it did not matter whether I died.*"[11]

7. Stringfellow, *Second Birthday*, 185, 187.
8. Stringfellow, *Second Birthday*, 187.
9. Stringfellow, *Politics of Spirituality*, 89 (italics original).
10. Stringfellow, *Politics of Spirituality*, 89.
11. Stringfellow, *Second Birthday*, 203 (italics original).

"Life," he said, "is a gift which death does not vitiate or void
... It is freedom from moral bondage to death that enables a man
to live humanly and to die at any moment without concern."[12]

## Ivan Illich

We have no comparable personal record from Illich about his pain.
However, David Cayley, in his introduction to his conversations
with Illich, tells the story of his suffering, which suggests that Illich
and Stringfellow were drinking from the same well. In fact, Illich
knew of Stringfellow's experience. His close friend Lee Hoinacki
showed him what Stringfellow had written about "The Ambiguity
of Pain," one of the sections in *A Second Birthday*. After reading,
Illich said of Stringfellow, "He knows what he's talking about."[13]

Though Illich did not seek biomedical care or surgery, he did
not ignore the tumor on his face. His obtained acupuncture, and
treated himself with yoga and smoking raw opium. The results of
these treatments were no better than Stringfellow's initial medical treatment, and he, like Stringfellow, was left with considerable
pain. He too needed to suffer.

Cayley describes that suffering this way:

> He had his own intuition, as he sometimes told me, that
> this was a cross that he should not try to avoid bearing
> ... Illich simply accepted his affliction as his share in
> Christ's suffering ... Illich lived what he believed: that
> each person is given a story to tell, and that nothing could
> be worse than to allow that unique story to be shrunk to
> a "survival rate" or reduced to an assigned "role" ... he
> treated even his suffering as a gift, and he made more of
> it than I could have imagined was possible before I met
> him. He had written in *Medical Nemesis* that "medical
> civilization" tries to "abolish the need for an art of suf-
> fering" and produces "a progressive flattening out of per-
> sonal virtuous performance." In his last two decades he

12. Stringfellow, *Second Birthday*, 203.
13. Quoted in Hoinacki, *Death*, 103.

got to cultivate this art and to give such a performance. He did it with good humor, great generosity with his time and counsel, expansive enjoyment of life's pleasures, and a growing sweetness in which whatever was left of a great man's pride seemed simply to burn away. By the end, he had drained his cup to the last drop and one morning laid down and peacefully died. No one who knew him well would have dared to say that he died "of cancer."[14]

## My Story

Since I wrote the first edition of this book, I have had the opportunity to apply the stories of Stringfellow and Illich to myself. I too am dying. Several years ago I had a routine prostatectomy, which to my dismay was followed by a year of symptoms I thought would have been dealt with by the removal of my prostate. Investigations eventually revealed the cause: prostate cancer, already spread to several bones. And then, like Stringfellow, I had a second birthday. Hormone therapy resulted in a nearly symptom-free remission lasting almost two years.

I knew this was not a cure but still found myself surprised, and almost offended, that the medical literature called my treatments "palliative care," a term I had associated with stopping chemotherapy and starting morphine. I had already decided against chemotherapy, and had few symptoms that needed relief. My hormone therapy was palliative in the sense that it did not cure me, but this palliation was far more than the stereotyped sad smiles and earnest assurances that it's okay to die. This was a remission that allowed me to work and travel and write and rewrite and record a podcast and publish. It was a time that taught me, in Stringfellow's words, "Life is a gift which death does not vitiate or void . . . It is freedom from moral bondage to death that enables a man to live humanly and to die at any moment without concern."[15]

---

14. Illich, *Rivers*, 38–40.
15. Stringfellow, *Second Birthday*, 203.

Then, as my remission began faltering, and the stories I had collected about Stringfellow and Illich over a decade earlier became very personal. I could not whitewash the pain. Biomedicine had only postponed it—for which I remain very grateful—but could not "abolish the need for an art of suffering."[16] Suffering, to repeat, is not the same as pain. Suffering is how I carry the pain. I am grateful for any medicine which can reduce pain, but I still need to carry the pain which medicine cannot remove.

As for a "personal virtuous performance" of this art of suffering, I have little confidence that my performance will be anything more than a flop.

I could be a first grader performing onstage for the first time. He climbs the stage and looks out at the cloud of witnesses, and he freezes. The crowd is expectant; his mind is blank. His lip quivers—then from offstage a whisper of his first line. He begins in a monotone; he has forgotten all his hand motions. He starts putting them in—a sweep of the arm, an extended hand—in all the wrong places. The cloud of witnesses twitters and he stammers. He looks down and sees Mommy, hugging him with her smile. Somehow he finishes.

His performance is a flop: he knows that. He is already crying by the time he gets back to his seat. That's when Daddy scoops him up and perches him on his shoulders—the best seat in the house.

## The Ultimate and the Necessary

What these stories demonstrate, I hope, is that nothing *ultimately* depends on the power of biomedicine. There is no question about whether or not biomedicine actually has power: it does, as Stringfellow's experience demonstrates, and as we showed in Chapters 3–5, and as my story confirms. That, incidentally, is why I could write all this and still remain a practicing doctor. That power is not the power to name what is going on, but it is power to modify the mechanisms of illness. Stringfellow opted for that power as a

16. Illich, *Rivers*, 39.

*part* of the way he dealt with his illness; I have learned to use a bit of that power as a *part* of the way I treat illness, and I opted for it in treating myself. As my remission began to fade, I was left with an overwhelming gratitude for life. Not a greed for more life but gratitude for every one of my seventy years.

But biomedicine is only a part, and it is not *necessary*. There is no technological imperative. Illich died at age seventy-six; would he have lived longer if he had had surgery? Or with surgery might he have died sooner? He understood his disease as an opportunity to share in Christ's suffering—not an understanding I would ever want to remove. Stringfellow likewise understood biomedicine as an option, but not *necessary*: he was free from anxiety, and knew it didn't matter if he died, knew this *before* the biomedical intervention. By the time he underwent surgery, he had already been healed.

# Bibliography

Arbour, Mary Catherine. Entry for April 13, 2007. In an unpublished personal journal.

Berry, Wendell. "Health Is Membership." Speech delivered at a conference on Spirituality and Healing, Louisville, Kentucky, October 17, 1994. http://tipiglen.co.uk/berryhealth.html/.

Blanchard, Michael Kelly. "'The Holy Land of the Broken Heart' (also called "The Hope That Ends the Human Drought"). Track 4 on *Mercy in the Maze*. Nashville: Diadem Music 7-90113-104-7, 1991.

Downing, Raymond. *Biohealth: Beyond Medicalization; Imposing Health*. Eugene, OR: Pickwick Publications, 2011.

Dubos, René Jules. *Mirage of Health: Utopias, Progress and Biological Change*. New Brunswick, NJ: Rutgers University Press, 1987.

Duden, Barbara. "Ivan Illich: Beyond *Medical Nemesis* (1976); The Search for Modernity's Disembodiment of 'I' and 'You.'" Notes for the Bremen Symposium *Ivan Illich zum Abschied* Feb 7–8, 2003. Translated by Jan Lambertz.

———. "The Quest for Past Somatics." In *The Challenges of Ivan Illich*, edited by Lee Hoinacki and Carl Mitcham, 219–30. Albany: State University of New York Press, 2002.

Eliot, T. S. *Four Quartets*. New York: Harcourt Brace Jovanovich, 1971.

Ellul, Jacques. "Biblical Positions on Medicine." Translated by Lisa Richmond. *Ellul Forum* 59 (2017) 3–7.

———. *The Presence of the Kingdom*. Translated by Olive Wyon. New York: Seabury, 1967.

———. *The Technological Society*. Translated by John Wilkinson. New York: Vintage, 1964.

———. *Violence: Reflections from a Christian Perspective*. Translated by Cecelia Gaul Kings. London: Mowbrays, 1978.

Gallagher, E. John, et al. "Effectiveness of Bystander Cardiopulmonary Resuscitation and Survival Following Out-of-Hospital Cardiac Arrest." *Journal of the American Medical Association* 274/24 (1995) 1922–25.

Hadler, Nortin M. *The Last Well Person: How to Stay Well Despite the Health-Care System*. Montreal: McGill-Queen's University Press, 2004.

Hoinacki, Lee. *Dying Is Not Death*. Eugene, OR: Resource Publications, 2007.

Illich, Ivan. "Brave New Biocracy: Health Care from Womb to Tomb." *New Perspective Quarterly* 11/1 (1994) 4–12.

———. "Health as One's Own Responsibility: No, Thank You!" *Journal of Consciousness Studies* 1/1 (1994) 25–31.

———. *Medical Nemesis: The Expropriation of Health*. New York: Pantheon, 1976.

———. "L'obsession de la santé parfaite." *Manière de voir* 73/2 (2004) 031. **[KC: pgs]**

———. *The Rivers North of the Future: The Testament of Ivan Illich*. As told to David Cayley. Foreword by Charles Taylor. Toronto: House of Anansi, 2011.

Kleinman, Arthur. *The Illness Narratives: Suffering, Healing, and the Human Condition*. New York: Basic Books, 1988.

Lewis, C. S. *The Chronicles of Narnia*. New York: Harper Collins, 2001.

———. *Mere Christianity*. Rev. and enl. ed., with a new introduction. New York: Macmillan, 1977.

Magesa, Laurenti. *African Religion: The Moral Traditions of Abundant Life*. Maryknoll, NY: Orbis, 1997.

Murphy, Donald J., et al. "The Influence of the Probability of Survival on Patients' Preferences Regarding Cardiopulmonary Resuscitation." *New England Journal of Medicine* 330 (1994) 545–49.

Nouwen, Henri J. M. *The Wounded Healer: Ministry in Contemporary Society*. Garden City, NY: Doubleday, 1972.

Rolheiser, Ronald. *The Holy Longing: The Search for a Christian Spirituality*. New York: Doubleday, 1999.

Sontag, Susan. *Illness as Metaphor and AIDS and Its Metaphors*. New York: Picador, 2001.

Starfield, Barbara. "Is US Health Really the Best in the World?" *Journal of the American Medical Association* 284/4 (2000) 483–85.

Stringfellow, William. *An Ethic for Christians and Other Aliens in a Strange Land*. Waco: Word, 1973.

———. *An Ethic for Christians and Other Aliens in a Strange Land*. The William Stringfellow Library. The Ethics Trilogy. Eugene, OR: Wipf & Stock, 2004.

———. *Instead of Death*. New and exp. ed. The William Stringfellow Library. The Ethics Trilogy. Eugene, OR: Wipf & Stock, 2004.

———. "Introduction." In *The Presence of the Kingdom*, by Jacques Ellul, 1–6. Translated by Olive Wyon. New York: Seabury, 1967.

———. *The Politics of Spirituality*. The William Stringfellow Library. The Dissent Trilogy. Eugene, OR: Wipf & Stock, 2006.

———. *A Second Birthday: A Personal Confrontation with Illness, Pain, and Death*. The William Stringfellow Library. The Autobiographical Triology. Eugene, OR: Wipf & Stock, 2005.